WORLD
HISTORY SERIES

The Fall of Vietnam

WORLD
HISTORY SERIES

The Fall of
Vietnam

Titles in the World History Series

WORLD HISTORY SERIES

The Fall of Vietnam

by
Philip Gavin

LUCENT
BOOKS®

THOMSON
™
GALE

San Diego • Detroit • New York • San Francisco • Cleveland • New Haven, Conn. • Waterville, Maine • London • Munich

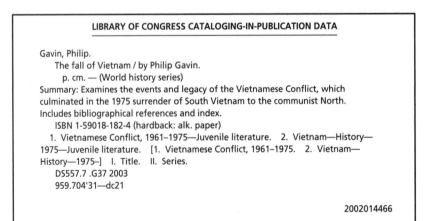

On cover: Vietnamese citizens scramble to board a U.S. helicopter during an evacuation of South Vietnam in 1975.

© 2003 by Lucent Books. Lucent Books is an imprint of The Gale Group, Inc., a division of Thomson Learning, Inc.

Lucent Books® and Thomson Learning™ are trademarks used herein under license.

For more information, contact
Lucent Books
27500 Drake Rd.
Farmington Hills, MI 48331-3535
Or you can visit our Internet site at http://www.gale.com

LIBRARY OF CONGRESS CATALOGING-IN-PUBLICATION DATA

Gavin, Philip.
   The fall of Vietnam / by Philip Gavin.
     p. cm. — (World history series)
  Summary: Examines the events and legacy of the Vietnamese Conflict, which culminated in the 1975 surrender of South Vietnam to the communist North.
  Includes bibliographical references and index.
    ISBN 1-59018-182-4 (hardback: alk. paper)
   1. Vietnamese Conflict, 1961–1975—Juvenile literature. 2. Vietnam—History—1975—Juvenile literature. [1. Vietnamese Conflict, 1961–1975. 2. Vietnam—History—1975–] I. Title. II. Series.
    DS557.7 .G37 2003
    959.704'31—dc21

                            2002014466

Printed in the United States of America

Contents

2689

Foreword

Each year on the first day of school, nearly every history teacher faces the task of explaining why his or her students should study history. One logical answer to this question is that exploring what happened in our past explains how the things we often take for granted—our customs, ideas, and institutions—came to be. As statesman and historian Winston Churchill put it, "Every nation or group of nations has its own tale to tell. Knowledge of the trials and struggles is necessary to all who would comprehend the problems, perils, challenges, and opportunities which confront us today." Thus, a study of history puts modern ideas and institutions in perspective. For example, though the founders of the United States were talented and creative thinkers, they clearly did not invent the concept of democracy. Instead, they adapted some democratic ideas that had originated in ancient Greece and with which the Romans, the British, and others had experimented. An exploration of these cultures, then, reveals their very real connection to us through institutions that continue to shape our daily lives.

Another reason often given for studying history is the idea that lessons exist in the past from which contemporary societies can benefit and learn. This idea, although controversial, has always been an intriguing one for historians. Those who agree that society can benefit from the past often quote philosopher George Santayana's famous statement, "Those who cannot remember the past are condemned to repeat it." Historians who subscribe to Santayana's philosophy believe that, for example, studying the events that led up to the major world wars or other significant historical events would allow society to chart a different and more favorable course in the future.

Just as difficult as convincing students to realize the importance of studying history is the search for useful and interesting supplementary materials that present historical events in a context that can be easily understood. The volumes in Lucent Books' World History series attempt to present a broad, balanced, and penetrating view of the march of history. Ancient Egypt's important wars and rulers, for example, are presented against the rich and colorful backdrop of Egyptian religious, social, and cultural developments. The series engages the reader by enhancing historical events with these cultural contexts. For example, in *Ancient Greece,* the text covers the role of women in that society. Slavery is discussed in *The Roman Empire,* as well as how slaves earned their freedom. The numerous and varied aspects of everyday life in these and other societies are explored in each volume of the series. Additionally, the series covers the major political, cultural, and philosophical ideas as the torch of civilization is passed from ancient Mesopotamia and Egypt, through Greece, Rome, Medieval Europe, and other world cultures, to the modern day.

The material in the series is formatted in a thorough, precise, and organized manner. Each volume offers the reader a comprehensive and clearly written overview of an important historical event or period. The topic under discussion is placed in a broad, historical context. For example, *The Renaissance* begins with a discussion of the High Middle Ages and the loss of central control that allowed certain Italian cities to develop artistically. The book ends by looking forward to the Reformation and interpreting the societal changes that grew out of the Renaissance. Thus, students are not only involved in a historical era, but also enveloped by the events leading up to that era and the events following it.

One important and unique feature in the World History series is the primary and secondary source quotations that richly supplement each volume. These quotes are useful in a number of ways. First, they allow students access to sources they would not normally be exposed to because of the difficulty and obscurity of the original source. The quotations range from interesting anecdotes to farsighted cultural perspectives and are drawn from historical witnesses both past and present. Second, the quotes demonstrate how and where historians themselves derive their information on the past as they strive to reach a consensus on historical events. Lastly, all of the quotes are footnoted, familiarizing students with the citation process and allowing them to verify quotes and/or look up the original source if the quote piques their interest.

Finally, the books in the World History series provide a detailed launching point for further research. Each book contains a bibliography specifically geared toward student research. A second, annotated bibliography introduces students to all the sources the author consulted when compiling the book. A chronology of important dates gives students an overview, at a glance, of the topic covered. Where applicable, a glossary of terms is included.

In short, the series is designed not only to acquaint readers with the basics of history, but also to make them aware that their lives are a part of an ongoing human saga. Perhaps they will then come to the same realization as famed historian Arnold Toynbee. In his monumental work, *A Study of History*, he wrote about becoming aware of history flowing through him in a mighty current, and of his own life "welling like a wave in the flow of this vast tide."

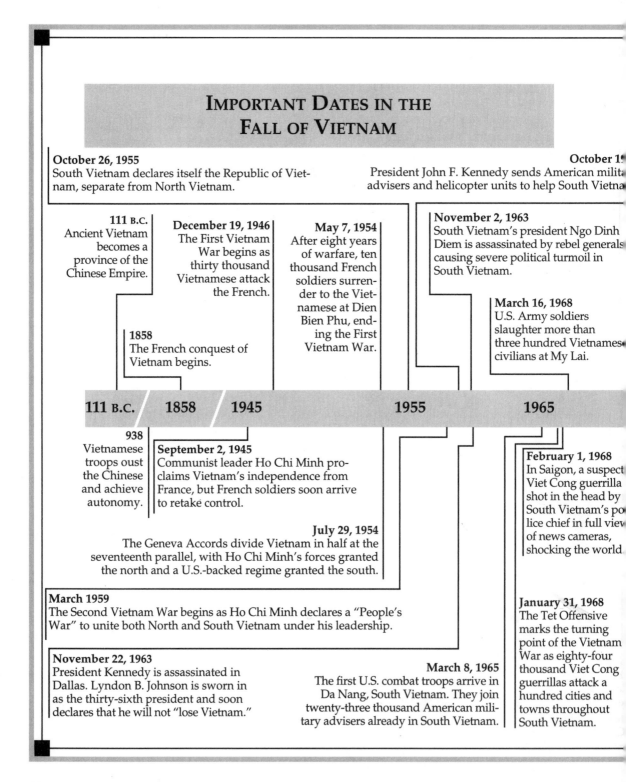

IMPORTANT DATES IN THE FALL OF VIETNAM

October 26, 1955
South Vietnam declares itself the Republic of Vietnam, separate from North Vietnam.

October 1...
President John F. Kennedy sends American milit... advisers and helicopter units to help South Vietna...

111 B.C.
Ancient Vietnam becomes a province of the Chinese Empire.

December 19, 1946
The First Vietnam War begins as thirty thousand Vietnamese attack the French.

May 7, 1954
After eight years of warfare, ten thousand French soldiers surrender to the Vietnamese at Dien Bien Phu, ending the First Vietnam War.

November 2, 1963
South Vietnam's president Ngo Dinh Diem is assassinated by rebel generals causing severe political turmoil in South Vietnam.

March 16, 1968
U.S. Army soldiers slaughter more than three hundred Vietnames... civilians at My Lai.

1858
The French conquest of Vietnam begins.

| 111 B.C. | 1858 | 1945 | 1955 | 1965 |

938
Vietnamese troops oust the Chinese and achieve autonomy.

September 2, 1945
Communist leader Ho Chi Minh proclaims Vietnam's independence from France, but French soldiers soon arrive to retake control.

February 1, 1968
In Saigon, a suspect... Viet Cong guerrilla shot in the head by South Vietnam's po... lice chief in full view of news cameras, shocking the world.

July 29, 1954
The Geneva Accords divide Vietnam in half at the seventeenth parallel, with Ho Chi Minh's forces granted the north and a U.S.-backed regime granted the south.

March 1959
The Second Vietnam War begins as Ho Chi Minh declares a "People's War" to unite both North and South Vietnam under his leadership.

January 31, 1968
The Tet Offensive marks the turning point of the Vietnam War as eighty-four thousand Viet Cong guerrillas attack a hundred cities and towns throughout South Vietnam.

November 22, 1963
President Kennedy is assassinated in Dallas. Lyndon B. Johnson is sworn in as the thirty-sixth president and soon declares that he will not "lose Vietnam."

March 8, 1965
The first U.S. combat troops arrive in Da Nang, South Vietnam. They join twenty-three thousand American military advisers already in South Vietnam.

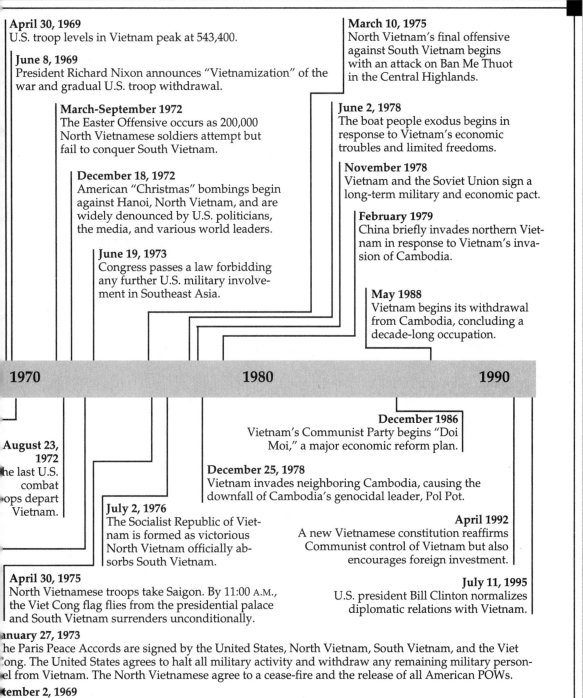

April 30, 1969
U.S. troop levels in Vietnam peak at 543,400.

June 8, 1969
President Richard Nixon announces "Vietnamization" of the war and gradual U.S. troop withdrawal.

March-September 1972
The Easter Offensive occurs as 200,000 North Vietnamese soldiers attempt but fail to conquer South Vietnam.

December 18, 1972
American "Christmas" bombings begin against Hanoi, North Vietnam, and are widely denounced by U.S. politicians, the media, and various world leaders.

June 19, 1973
Congress passes a law forbidding any further U.S. military involvement in Southeast Asia.

March 10, 1975
North Vietnam's final offensive against South Vietnam begins with an attack on Ban Me Thuot in the Central Highlands.

June 2, 1978
The boat people exodus begins in response to Vietnam's economic troubles and limited freedoms.

November 1978
Vietnam and the Soviet Union sign a long-term military and economic pact.

February 1979
China briefly invades northern Vietnam in response to Vietnam's invasion of Cambodia.

May 1988
Vietnam begins its withdrawal from Cambodia, concluding a decade-long occupation.

1970　　　　**1980**　　　　**1990**

August 23, 1972
The last U.S. combat troops depart Vietnam.

July 2, 1976
The Socialist Republic of Vietnam is formed as victorious North Vietnam officially absorbs South Vietnam.

April 30, 1975
North Vietnamese troops take Saigon. By 11:00 A.M., the Viet Cong flag flies from the presidential palace and South Vietnam surrenders unconditionally.

January 27, 1973
The Paris Peace Accords are signed by the United States, North Vietnam, South Vietnam, and the Viet Cong. The United States agrees to halt all military activity and withdraw any remaining military personnel from Vietnam. The North Vietnamese agree to a cease-fire and the release of all American POWs.

September 2, 1969
Ho Chi Minh dies of a heart attack at age seventy-nine. He is succeeded by Le Duan.

December 1986
Vietnam's Communist Party begins "Doi Moi," a major economic reform plan.

December 25, 1978
Vietnam invades neighboring Cambodia, causing the downfall of Cambodia's genocidal leader, Pol Pot.

April 1992
A new Vietnamese constitution reaffirms Communist control of Vietnam but also encourages foreign investment.

July 11, 1995
U.S. president Bill Clinton normalizes diplomatic relations with Vietnam.

Centuries of Strife

At noon on April 30, 1975, a column of tanks commanded by troops from North Vietnam smashed open the gates of South Vietnam's presidential palace in Saigon. South Vietnam's leader broadcast a message of total surrender. The surrender of South Vietnam to North Vietnam in 1975 marked a turning point in the two-thousand-year struggle by the Vietnamese people against outsiders and among themselves over the fate of their country. Through so many centuries, the Vietnamese people had successfully joined together to fight off various foreign invaders. But time and time again, they had also descended into bitter fighting among themselves.

The first recorded conquest of Vietnam was by Imperial China in 111 B.C. For the next thousand years, Vietnam existed only as a province of China. Although the Vietnamese greatly admired the Chinese and incorporated much of China's culture into their own, they also yearned for independence. By the year 938, the Vietnamese had mustered enough strength to assert their independence. Troops led by General Ngo Quyen defeated the Chinese in a battle in northern Vietnam near present-day Haiphong. Before the battle, General Ngo's troops placed metal-tipped spikes in the water all along the tidal riverbed at Bach Dang. At high tide, when the spikes were underwater and could not be seen, the Vietnamese lured all of the Chinese boats into battle. As the tide receded, the Chinese boats became entangled in the spikes and were easily destroyed by the Vietnamese.

THE FRENCH TAKE VIETNAM

For nearly nine hundred years, Vietnam maintained a measure of autonomy, punctuated by periods of domination by China. Vietnam's independence ended altogether in the nineteenth century when France established colonies in Southeast Asia, backed by the might of the French military. The conquest of Vietnam by the French began in 1858 with the capture of Tourane (present-day Da Nang) in central Vietnam. Saigon and surrounding areas in the south were the next to be taken. Finally, in 1883 the French navy bombarded the imperial capitol of Hue, forcing the Vietnamese to sign a treaty granting France control over the entire country.

Vietnam had once again lost its independence. Many Vietnamese quietly accepted their role as French subjects, but others refused to be subjugated and fought back by using hit-and-run tactics. A French military commander commented on the problems his men faced in dealing with the elusive jungle guerrillas: "We have had enormous difficulties in enforcing our authority. . . . [The Vietnamese guerrillas] appear from nowhere in large numbers, destroy everything, and then disappear into nowhere."[1]

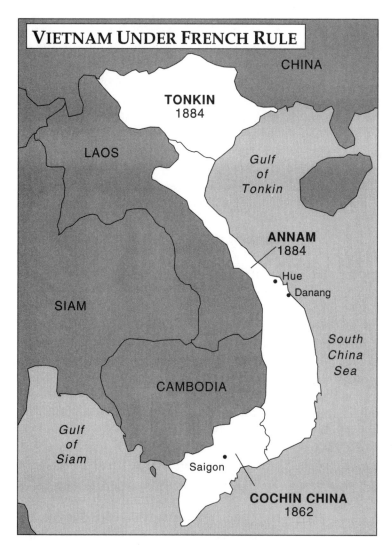

VIETNAM UNDER FRENCH RULE

CHINA

TONKIN
1884

LAOS

Gulf
of
Tonkin

ANNAM
1884

Hue
Danang

SIAM

South
China
Sea

CAMBODIA

Gulf
of
Siam

Saigon

COCHIN CHINA
1862

The French engaged in brutal retaliation for the attacks. They destroyed any village they thought was harboring guerrillas and shot or beheaded village leaders. Using such drastic methods, the French were able to quash the Vietnamese resistance and by the early 1900s considered Vietnam to be pacified.

"HE WHO ENLIGHTENS"

Peace, however, was short-lived. France itself had been conquered by Nazi Germany, and in 1940, as part of its attempt to dominate all of Asia, Germany's ally, Japan, invaded Vietnam. For the next five years, the French colonial authorities, collaborating with the Japanese, shared control of Vietnam. In March 1945, amid rumors of a possible American invasion and suspicious of the colonists' allegiances, the Japanese ousted the French altogether and seized complete control of Vietnam. But by this time, Japan's armed forces throughout the South Pacific had experienced a string of military defeats at the hands of the United States and its allies. In August 1945, after the United States dropped atomic bombs on two Japanese cities, Japan surrendered.

Under the terms of the peace treaty, Japan lost control of all of its conquered possessions, including Vietnam.

During this tumultuous period, a new leader named Ho Chi Minh emerged in Vietnam. Ho was a Communist who led a powerful organization called the Viet Minh (Vietnam Independence League). His goal was to establish a fully independent Vietnam, led by the Vietnamese Communist Party. However, Ho Chi Minh and his followers faced a huge problem: With the ending of World War II, the French made it known that they intended to keep Vietnam as a colony.

Ho and his followers strongly opposed the idea of French recolonization of their homeland, and on September 2, 1945, Ho Chi Minh formally declared Vietnam's independence. Hostilities quickly erupted when French soldiers came ashore to forcibly reestablish colonial rule. In the port of Haiphong, near Hanoi, shooting broke out, followed by house-to-house fighting between French troops and the Viet Minh. French warships retaliated by shelling Haiphong while French infantry and armored units attacked, routing the Viet Minh. As French troops moved inland to occupy Hanoi, Ho Chi Minh and his Viet Minh fighters abandoned the city and retreated into the surrounding jungle.

No country granted diplomatic recognition to Ho Chi Minh's government, but Ho did not abandon his efforts to gain Vietnam's independence. Amid the relative safety of their jungle sanctuary, Ho's Viet Minh fighters gathered any weapons they could find, from antique muskets to stolen French and Japanese rifles, and bided their time. Then, on December 19, 1946, Viet Minh military commander Vo Nguyen Giap sounded the call for a violent uprising against the French: "Sacrifice to the last drop of blood in the struggle for the Independence and Unification of the Fatherland. The resistance will be long and extremely hard, but the just cause is on our side, and we will be victorious."[2]

THE FIRST VIETNAM WAR

Giap's call to arms marked the beginning of an eight-year struggle in which the Vietnamese, bolstered by additional weapons provided by the People's Republic of China, repeatedly attacked French military outposts. Each time the Viet Minh attacked, they suffered heavy losses. Sometimes, during a single encounter with the French, up to five or six thousand Viet Minh soldiers were killed. Ho Chi Minh, though, believed that such drastic casualties were acceptable and boldly predicted victory in spite of them: "We may lose ten Vietnamese for every Frenchman, but in the end we will win."[3]

By late 1953, numerous large and small battles had been fought in northern Vietnam. With casualties mounting and no end to the bloody conflict in sight, the French chose a daring maneuver to improve their strategic position. In the nearly impenetrable jungles of northwest Vietnam at the frontier village of Dien Bien Phu, they built a small air base, which they surrounded with several fortified outposts. The French intended to use Dien Bien Phu as a staging point from which they could strike at the Viet Minh's rear areas. The Vietnamese observed this in amazement, sensing that the French had made a huge blunder in choosing such an isolated location. Hop-

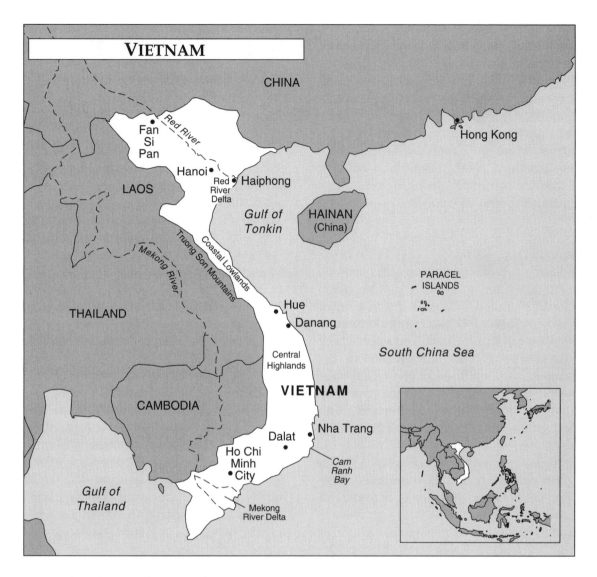

VIETNAM

CHINA

Fan
Si
Pan

Red River

Hong Kong

Hanoi

Red
River
Delta

Haiphong

LAOS

Gulf of
Tonkin

HAINAN
(China)

Coastal Lowlands

Truong Son Mountains

Mekong River

THAILAND

PARACEL
ISLANDS

Hue

Danang

Central
Highlands

South China Sea

VIETNAM

CAMBODIA

Nha Trang

Dalat

Ho Chi
Minh
City

Cam
Ranh
Bay

Gulf of
Thailand

Mekong
River Delta

ing to knock out the French in one colossal blow, the Vietnamese decided to mount a mass attack. Not realizing the danger their forces were in, the French kept the bulk of their troops in central Vietnam, assigned to other duties; French forces at Dien Bien Phu were thus outnumbered five to one.

What came to be known as the Battle of Dien Bien Phu erupted on March 13, 1954, as fifty thousand Viet Minh soldiers attacked ten thousand dug-in Frenchmen in their fortified outposts. Intense shelling by the Vietnamese quickly rendered the French air base unusable. With their landing strip unavailable, the French were unable to get adequate reinforcements or badly needed supplies of ammunition, water, and medicines. The Viet Minh overran the outlying outposts one by one, edging closer to the air base and the French command post.

The French sent out desperate appeals for help to the United States. However, U.S. president Dwight D. Eisenhower, unwilling to commit American troops to a seemingly hopeless cause, took no action. After holding out for several weeks, the entire French force at Dien Bien Phu surrendered on May 7, 1954. Following its disastrous defeat, the French military withdrew completely from Vietnam, thus ending the First Vietnam War.

UNSETTLED AFTERMATH

With the French gone, Ho Chi Minh thought he would be able to unite all of Vietnam under his leadership. However, he soon ran into serious obstacles. Many Vietnamese in the southern part of the country had benefited from French rule, which had afforded the south considerable autonomy. These southerners, who had grown wealthy during the French colonial era, were strongly anti-Communist and had no desire to be ruled by Ho Chi Minh and his fellow Communists. Tempers soon flared between northern and southern Vietnamese. Political leaders from around the world watched in dismay, worried that this quarrel might descend into armed conflict.

To ease tensions, in July 1954 a temporary solution was worked out during an international political conference in Geneva, Switzerland. According to the plan, countrywide elections to choose a national leader would be held within two years. For the time being, however, Vietnam would be divided in half along the seventeenth parallel, with Ho Chi Minh and his Communists granted control of the north and a non-Communist government granted control of the south.

In the south, an ardent anti-Communist named Ngo Dinh Diem became the leader. The United States, as part of its efforts to halt the spread of communism in Asia, decided to support Diem. Fearing a victory by Ho Chi Minh and the Communists and with the blessing of the United States, Diem postponed the scheduled elections in the south.

But a divided Vietnam could not live in peace indefinitely. Diem himself predicted that "another more deadly war"[4] concerning the country's future would soon erupt. His pessimistic prediction proved accurate in 1959 as Ho Chi Minh set out to unite Vietnam by force. To prevent a takeover of the south by the Communists, the United States sent in military advisers and supplies to aid the newly formed South Vietnamese army. But the south's forces fared poorly against battle-hardened Communists who saw themselves as fighting for Vietnam's independence. As the conflict escalated, American advisers and facilities in South Vietnam came under direct attack. This led to a momentous decision in February 1965 by U.S. president Lyndon B. Johnson to send American combat troops into South Vietnam. What had started as a civil conflict between the Vietnamese had now blossomed into an American war.

1 The American War

The war in Vietnam would turn out to be the longest and most frustrating conflict America had ever been involved in. U.S. combat soldiers began arriving in South Vietnam in March 1965 and soon found themselves under fire in much the same way the French had. And just as they had done in their struggle with the French, Ho Chi Minh and his military commanders were confident they could defeat the Americans with a combination of guerrilla warfare and conventional battle tactics.

VIET CONG METHODS

U.S. soldiers were routinely attacked by Communist guerrilla fighters known as the Viet Cong (VC). The elusive VC were expert at using Vietnam's jungle cover to their advantage. They would patiently wait until American patrols came within striking distance and then attack. As quickly as they appeared, they would vanish. The Viet Cong were so effective at concealing themselves that some American soldiers completed a yearlong tour of combat duty without once seeing their enemy. One U.S. veteran recalls,

> It was eerie . . . . We called the Viet Cong ghosts in my platoon . . . . You

never saw them. You'd see a shot of flame as they'd shoot at you. You might see a shadow, very rarely. But they seemed to be capable of incredible things . . . of supernatural sorts of things. So we thought and so it seemed. And an image of the enemy began to grow of an enemy capable of the most incredible sorts of deeds.[5]

To escape detection, VC guerrilla units built an extensive network of underground tunnels, many of which extended under the countryside for miles. In addition to emerging from the tunnels to conduct hit-and-run raids, the Viet Cong would plant numerous mines in fields and roads, taking a heavy toll on patrolling American troops. Sneaking into South Vietnam's cities, the VC also planted time bombs at places frequented by Americans and committed sabotage such as blowing up fuel depots.

Other specially trained VC became political assassins, targeting fellow Vietnamese who cooperated with the Americans. One captured VC operative revealed during his interrogation,

> When we'd get an order to kill someone, we'd begin keeping tabs on that person's activities. We would also set

Viet Cong Oath of Honor

Upon joining the Viet Cong, new recruits took this all-encompassing Oath of Honor, reprinted here from Inside the VC and the NVA: The Real Story of North Vietnam's Armed Forces, *by Michael Lee Lanning and Dan Cragg.*

1. I swear I am prepared to sacrifice all for Vietnam. I will fight to my last breath against imperialism, colonialism, Vietnamese traitors, and aggression in order to make Vietnam independent, democratic and united.

2. I swear to obey absolutely all orders from my commanders, executing them wholeheartedly, promptly, and accurately.

3. I swear to fight firmly for the people without complaint and without becoming discouraged even if life is hard or dangerous. I will go forward in combat without fear, will never retreat regardless of suffering involved.

4. I swear to learn to fight better and shape myself into a true revolutionary soldier battling the invading American imperialists and their servants, seeking to make Vietnam democratic, wealthy and strong.

5. I swear to preserve organizational secrecy, and to keep secret my unit's plans, the name of my unit commander, and all secrets of other revolutionary units.

6. I swear, if taken by the enemy, I will not reveal any information even under inhuman torture. I will remain faithful to the Revolution and not be bribed by the enemy.

7. I swear in the name of unity to love my friends in my unit as myself, to work cooperatively with them in combat and at all other times.

8. I swear to maintain and protect my weapons, ensuring they are never damaged or captured by the enemy.

9. I swear that in my relationships with the people I will do three things and eschew three things. I will respect, protect, and help the people; I will not steal from, threaten nor inconvenience the people. I will do all things to win their confidence.

10. I swear to indulge in self-criticism, to be a model solider of the Revolution, and never to harm either the Liberation Army or Vietnam.

up a network of agents inside the area where the assassination was supposed to take place to give us an understanding of the everyday goings on there . . . . After we had understood everything thoroughly, we would draw up an operation plan . . . . Altogether I participated in about thirty killings, mostly of [South Vietnamese] policemen and [village] chiefs.[6]

For American ground troops, efforts to find and destroy the Viet Cong were frustrating and futile. For one thing, the VC always wore civilian clothing and were therefore indistinguishable from other Vietnamese. One ex-Marine, who had seen several buddies killed by VC mines, said the guerrilla tactics led American troops to make some deadly assumptions about those they were supposed to be helping:

Women walk amidst the rubble left by a Viet Cong guerrilla attack.

You'd go out, you'd run a patrol. Somebody hits a mine. There's a couple of dead people . . . . And after a while you start thinking these [local village] people must know where the mines are—how come they never step on them? They must be VC. They must be VC sympathizers. And so, over a relatively short period of time, you begin to treat all of the Vietnamese as though they are the enemy. If you can't tell, you shoot first and ask questions later.[7]

Other times, the Americans found themselves in more traditional battle conditions. When the situation suited them, the highly disciplined uniformed soldiers of the North Vietnamese Army (NVA), using state-of-the-art combat gear provided by the People's Republic of China and the Soviet Union, would confront U.S. troops. These soldiers were every bit as motivated as their Viet Cong counterparts. Among these units, a man who killed three or more Americans would be decorated as a "valiant American killer."[8]

Whether in guerrilla or conventional warfare, NVA troops and the Viet Cong were usually defeated outright whenever they engaged American troops. Yet no matter how heavy their casualties, they always reappeared in strength days or weeks later, as a steady stream of soldiers and supplies flowed into South Vietnam from North Vietnam via the Ho Chi Minh Trail. This fifteen-hundred-mile-long network of dirt roads and jungle paths ran along the western border of Vietnam, winding in and out of neighboring Laos and Cambodia. Massive bombing of the trail by American airplanes failed to interrupt the flow of Communist soldiers

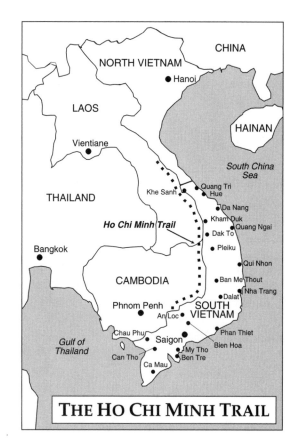

THE HO CHI MINH TRAIL

and materials into South Vietnam. The North Vietnamese would simply detour around damaged areas or quickly repair the damage.

CONFUSED BATTLE TACTICS

As time went on, it became clear that not only were the Americans and their South Vietnamese allies failing to break the fighting spirit of their enemy, but there seemed to be little progress, as measured by captured territory, toward winning the war. For the Americans, experimental battle tactics were partly to blame. Unlike in World War II or the Korean War, American troops did not advance along traditional battle lines and seize and hold territory. Instead, in Vietnam they used a new tactic in which soldiers were flown by helicopters into a battle zone to fight and then withdrawn to their base camps after the battle. Once they had gone, Viet Cong and North Vietnamese troops often came out of the jungle and reoccupied the territory the Americans had just left.

John Kerry, a decorated combat veteran who later became a U.S. senator, commented on the apparent futility of the military strategy he witnessed in action in Vietnam:

> A typical mission really didn't have any sense to it. The logic that was explained to us by the command in Vietnam was that we were "showing the flag in the backyard of the enemy." There were [soldiers] who believed that we were fighting Communism and that this was terrific and it was important and who were all swept up in it. But I think most people did not [believe that]. Most people began to see that we weren't gaining any territory. We weren't winning the hearts and minds of anybody. We certainly weren't securing any particular strongholds or strategic objec-

tives. We were simply doing a very macho kind of public demonstration of our presence.[9]

In America, frustration with such a strategy mounted as the war dragged on through 1966 and into 1967. The American

American soldiers search for the enemy in the Vietnamese jungle. During the war, soldiers employed nontraditional battle tactics in an effort to defeat the Viet Cong.

public plainly saw that, despite a death toll among American troops that was approaching one thousand per month, victory was nowhere in sight. Instead, President Johnson and his White House advisers were proceeding on the assumption that they could pressure North Vietnam into peace talks by showing them America's military might. Retired general Norman Schwarzkopf, who as a young officer served in Vietnam, observes, "Washington believed that if we killed more of them than they killed of us, they'd give up and not want to fight anymore. . . . We never really fought the war strategically."[10]

One of President Johnson's key advisers, Secretary of State Dean Rusk, later admitted that the American approach from the beginning had been to fight a limited war: "We did not want to expand the war into a war of total destruction. What we were trying to do was to keep the North Vietnamese from overrunning South Vietnam."[11] Rusk and Johnson's other White House advisers were hopeful that a political settlement similar to the one that ended the Korean War a decade earlier could be reached and that like Korea, Vietnam could be permanently divided into north and south.

But Ho Chi Minh and his supporters were resolved not to compromise. "Our people are determined to fight on. We will endure all sacrifice for ten years, 20 years or longer, until complete victory,"[12] Ho Chi Minh had declared after the first American combat troops set foot in Vietnam.

In spite of such avowals, President Johnson attempted to negotiate directly with Ho Chi Minh by sending him secret letters, such as one in 1967 in which he wrote,

I am writing to you in the hope that the conflict in Vietnam can be brought to an end. That conflict has already taken a heavy toll—in lives lost, in wounds inflicted, in property destroyed, and in simple human misery. If we fail to find a just and peaceful solution, history will judge us harshly. . . . There is one way to overcome this problem and to move forward in the search for a peaceful settlement. That is for us to arrange for direct talks between trusted representatives in a secure setting and away from the glare of publicity.[13]

Ho Chi Minh bluntly responded in a letter to Johnson: "The U.S. Government has unleashed the war of aggression in Vietnam. It must cease this aggression. . . . The Vietnamese people will never submit to force, they will never accept talks under threat of bombs."[14]

North Vietnam's refusal to negotiate upset the carefully laid plans of President Johnson and his White House advisers. They spent long hours pondering what to do next in Vietnam. Meanwhile, the Communists stepped up their attacks against American troops and military facilities throughout South Vietnam. Responding to this increased violence, Johnson authorized intensive aerial bombings of North Vietnam in a campaign called "Rolling Thunder." Continuous bombing also occurred throughout South Vietnam against suspected VC and NVA troop strongholds.

DISSENSION GROWS

The graphic TV news footage of the human destruction wrought by U.S. bombs

LEARNING TO KILL

The ease of death on the battlefield and the futility of war are revealed in this letter from George Olsen, U.S. Seventy-fifth Infantry (Ranger) Division, to a friend back in America, excerpted from Bernard Edelman's Dear America: Letters Home from Vietnam.

"Last Monday I went on my first hunter-killer operation and saw Mars [the god of war] close up for the first time. We had two teams—12 men, inserted at dawn about two miles inland and slightly north of Chu Lai about an [hour's ride on] the choppers. We set up around a trail, and a lone NVA officer walked into the middle of us. We tried for a POW [prisoner of war], but he panicked and took off in a blizzard of shells. I had him in my sights, threw three slugs at him and he just disappeared. No Hollywood theatrics—one minute he's a living, running human being, the next second he's down, just a red lump of clay. . . . [Later,] we found some huts the NVA had been working on, then moved out across a dried-up paddy when all hell broke loose. . . . The frightening thing about it all is that it is so very easy to kill in war. There's no remorse . . . not even any regrets. When it happens, you are more afraid [than] you've ever been in your life—my hands shook so much I had trouble reloading and it took a visible effort to perform each motion and control what would normally be called panic, but which, somehow, isn't. You're scared, really scared, and there's no thinking about it. You kill because [the enemy] is doing his best to kill you and you desperately want to live. . . . And suddenly the grenades aren't going off anymore, the weapons stop and, unbelievably fast it seems, it's all over and you're alive because someone else is either dead or so anxious to stay alive that he's run away and you are the victor—if there is such a thing in war."

(Note: Olsen was killed in action on March 3, 1970.)

greatly upset many Americans at home. Members of the clergy, including renowned civil rights leader the Reverend Martin Luther King Jr., began to speak out against the war. In April 1967, King called for an end to the war saying,

As I ponder the madness of Vietnam, my mind goes constantly to the people of the [Indochina] peninsula. I speak now not of the soldiers of each side. . .but simply of the people who have been living under the curse of war for almost three continuous decades. . . . Now they languish under our bombs and consider us—not their fellow Vietnamese—the real enemy. . . . Somehow this madness must cease. I speak as a child of God and brother to the suffering poor of Vietnam and the poor of America. . . . I speak as a citizen of the world, for the world, as it stands aghast at the path we have taken. I speak as an American to the leaders of my own nation. The great initiative in this war is ours. The initiative to stop must be ours.[15]

Large protests in which activists called for America to stop the war began occurring regularly in Washington and other major cities and on hundreds of college campuses. Most of the protesters viewed the Vietnam conflict as an internal matter, a civil war, among the Vietnamese themselves over the future of their country. This view contrasted sharply with Johnson's oft-stated position that the war was key to stopping the spread of communism.

At first, activists' calls for an end to the bombing campaign and a withdrawal of American troops seemed extreme both to American politicians and to mainstream journalists. Over time, however, many Americans began to question the wisdom of continued U.S. military involvement in Vietnam. Faced with widening opposition to the war and the possibility that this opposition could cost him reelection, President Johnson agonized over the future of America's involvement in Vietnam.

A widow in mourning holds a picture of her husband who was killed during the 1968 Tet Offensive.

The Surprise Tet Offensive

Johnson's thinking about Vietnam, along with that of many Americans, was changed forever by the events of early 1968 during Tet, the traditional Vietnamese holiday celebrating the Lunar New Year. Tet had always been the occasion for a countrywide cease-fire in Vietnam. But in January 1968, that tradition was broken as eighty-four thousand Viet Cong guerrillas attacked in a hundred cities and towns all over South Vietnam. What came to be known as the Tet Offensive was intended by the Communists to ignite a general uprising among sympathetic peasants throughout South Vietnam, resulting in the overthrow of the south's government and perhaps paving the way for a complete military victory.

For Americans in Vietnam and back home as well, Tet was a stunning surprise. Just two months earlier, President Johnson had assured the American public concerning the war: "We are inflicting greater losses than we're taking."[16] The American commander in Vietnam, General William Westmoreland, had expanded on this comment to predict victory: "We are making progress and we are winning."[17]

But with the beginning of the Tet Offensive, the press reports coming from Vietnam seemed to indicate that the exact opposite was true. President Johnson's secretary of defense, Clark Clifford, commented after the war, "The Tet Offensive was such a shocking event to the public and to the [White House] administration. It was so unexpected, and in the early days of the Tet Offensive, it was eminently successful. It looked like the bottom was dropping out."[18]

The main focus of the Communists' efforts was the city of Hue, which was a hugely symbolic target because it was the country's former capital. Some twelve thousand NVA and Viet Cong troops stormed and occupied the lightly defended city. They then began executing more than three thousand so-called enemies of the people, including local government officials, captured South Vietnamese army officers, and Catholic priests. American and South Vietnamese troops counterattacked and were forced to fight house by house, street by street, to retake the city.

All over South Vietnam, American and South Vietnamese troops successfully counterattacked the Viet Cong and NVA. By March 1968, two months after the start of the Tet Offensive, most of the Communists' early territorial gains had been completely reversed. In fact, from a military perspective, the Tet Offensive turned out to be an overwhelming failure for the Communists, as journalist Peter Scholl-Latour, who witnessed the events firsthand, points out:

> The Communists had expected the entire population of South Vietnam to rise up against the Americans in a mass revolt. Instead, the vast majority remained completely passive. The Viet Cong had banked on mass desertions by South Vietnamese troops, but in the end, not a single unit of the [south's] national army went over to the Communists. From a purely military standpoint, the 1968 Tet Offensive was a complete fiasco and a disastrous blow to Hanoi's hopes. The combat units of the [Viet Cong] which had taken so long to build up, were entirely wiped out.[19]

American marines crouch in the rubble of a citadel in the former capital city of Hue.

happening. Americans seemed to lose confidence, realizing that, despite repeated assurances from President Johnson and various military leaders that the war was being won, the end was nowhere in sight.

Voicing this sentiment was none other than highly esteemed TV news anchor Walter Cronkite. He returned from a visit to Saigon and announced on CBS, "We have been too often disappointed by the optimism of the American leaders, both in Vietnam and Washington, to have faith any longer in the silver linings they find in the darkest clouds. . . . For now it seems more certain than ever that the bloody experience of Vietnam is to end in a stalemate."[20]

Nevertheless, the Tet Offensive was a political success for the North Vietnamese. Virtually the entire effort to fight off the attackers had been recorded and broadcast on American television. Among average Americans, support for the war seriously eroded as they saw what was

General Westmoreland later acknowledged that Tet marked the point at which America began losing the Vietnam War. Westmoreland blamed the press for this turn of events, describing news coverage from Vietnam as "gloom and doom, which gave the American people the impression that Americans were being defeated on the battlefield."[21]

By the spring of 1968, the war's cost, in terms of death and destruction in Vietnam, was growing daily. Furthermore, although American troops in Vietnam were winning all of the big battles, they were making no progress at all toward winning the war. The lack of progress, President Johnson knew, could well mean the end of his political life when the election was held later that year.

THE DOWNFALL OF LYNDON JOHNSON

Johnson's fears of what the Vietnam War was doing to his popularity were confirmed by the results of the primary election held in New Hampshire on March 12, 1968. Fellow Democrat Eugene McCarthy, running on an antiwar platform, nearly beat the president, missing by just a few hundred votes. To have a challenger come so close to beating the incumbent in a primary election that Johnson had expected to win in a landslide was a clear indication of the president's sagging popularity. Johnson now faced the embarrassing prospect that he might not be nominated by his own political party to run for another term.

Opposition to the war grew even among Johnson's top advisers. The U.S. secretary of defense, Clark Clifford, carefully studied the entire situation and came to the conclusion that the United States should exit Vietnam. To convince Johnson of this, Clifford convened a White House meeting of a group—known as the "Wise Men"—whose advice Johnson trusted. At a luncheon attended by President Johnson on March 26, 1968, most members of the Wise Men

THE FIRST TV WAR

Vietnam was the first war ever fought without news censorship. Therefore, Americans watching TV had a front-row seat to a war ten thousand miles away. And many were greatly angered by what they saw, such as this CBS News report by Morley Safer from August 1965 and quoted in John Clark Pratt's Vietnam Voices: Perspectives in the War Years, 1941–1982, *describing the destruction of a suspected VC village by U.S. Marines.*

"After surrounding the village and receiving one burst of automatic fire from an unidentified direction, the marines poured in 3.5 rocket fire, 79 grenade launchers, and heavy and light machine-gun fire. The marines then moved in, proceeding first with cigarette lighters, then with flame throwers, to burn down an estimated 150 dwellings. I subsequently learned that a marine platoon on the right flank wounded three women and killed one child in a rocket barrage. The day's operations netted about four prisoners—old men. Two marines were wounded, both by their own fire, although this has been denied."

TWO SIDES, TWO POINTS OF VIEW

Determined to prevent a Communist takeover of South Vietnam, President Lyndon Johnson dispatched U.S. combat troops, realizing that young Americans would lose their lives as a result. This was the dilemma of Vietnam, as revealed in the following excerpt from a 1965 speech from the LBJ presidential archives (found on the U.S. State Department website):

> I do not find it easy to send the flower of our youth, our finest young men, into battle. I have seen them in a thousand streets, of a hundred towns, in every state in this union, working and laughing and building, and filled with hope and life. I think I know, too, how their mothers weep and how their families sorrow. . . . [But] the people of South Vietnam have fought for many long years . . . and we just cannot now dishonor our word, or abandon our commitment, or leave those who believed us and who trusted us, to the [Communist] terror and repression and murder that would follow.

Meanwhile, North Vietnam's leader, Ho Chi Minh, declared that his people would resist U.S. intervention, as this 1965 speech excerpt, which appears in Bernard B. Fall's *Ho Chi Minh on Revolution: Selected Writings, 1920–66*, reveals:

> We love peace but we are not afraid of war. We are resolved to drive away the U.S. aggressors and to defend the freedom, independence, and territorial integrity of our Fatherland. The people throughout our country are firmly confident that with their militant solidarity, valiant spirit, and creative wisdom, and with the sympathy and support of the world's peoples, they will certainly lead this great Resistance War to complete victory.

Determined to succeed against the Communists, President Lyndon Johnson continued the Vietnam War, losing the support of his advisers.

strongly advocated a U.S. withdrawal from Vietnam. Five days later, the president gave a TV speech in which he announced a partial bombing halt and also implored North Vietnam to begin peace talks. Johnson then concluded the speech with a surprise announcement: "I shall not seek, and I will not accept, the nomination of my party for another term as your President."[22]

By now, most Americans wanted an end to the war. The 1968 presidential election, therefore, revolved around who could best make that happen. The Republican presidential candidate, former vice president Richard Nixon, campaigned on a slogan of "peace with honor."[23] His Democratic opponent, Hubert Humphrey, also promised to work for peace but had to overcome the fact that he had formerly supported Johnson's failed Vietnam policies.

On November 5, 1968, Nixon narrowly defeated Humphrey in the presidential election. Nixon became the thirty-seventh U.S. president and the fifth president over the past twenty-three years who would have to cope with Vietnam. At his inauguration ceremony on January 20, 1969, Nixon declared, "The greatest honor history can bestow is the title of peacemaker. This honor now beckons America."[24] But for Nixon and America, peace in Vietnam would be a long time coming. Meanwhile, things would get a lot worse both in the jungles of Vietnam and in America.

Chapter

2 America Withdraws

Newly elected president Richard Nixon faced the enormous challenge of trying to fulfill his campaign promise to get America out of Vietnam. Nixon wanted to bring the U.S. troops home as swiftly as possible, but he also wanted to prevent a military victory by North Vietnam. America up till this time had never lost a war. Like Johnson, Nixon hoped to negotiate a resolution that would leave South Vietnam independent and allow the United States to depart Vietnam as an apparent winner.

BARGAINING FOR PEACE

The complicated task of bargaining for peace with the North Vietnamese began in January 1969 when representatives from the United States, South Vietnam, North Vietnam, and the Viet Cong agreed to meet in Paris. Time was on the side of the North Vietnamese. The Americans were eager to exit Vietnam; by contrast, the North Vietnamese were prepared to fight for however long it took to unite Vietnam under Communist rule. What the North Vietnamese hoped to get was peace terms that could leave open the possibility of an eventual military victory over the south.

President Nixon's first proposal included an offer to withdraw U.S. troops from South Vietnam, provided that the North Vietnamese also withdrew their forces. The North Vietnamese not only turned down Nixon's offer but countered with demands such as Communist participation in South Vietnam's government—something that neither the Americans nor the South Vietnamese were likely to accept. The peace talks became hopelessly deadlocked and an angry and frustrated Nixon threatened North Vietnam with a resumption of bombing. The North Vietnamese ignored these threats and continued to stall.

Meanwhile, Nixon decided the time had come to fulfill his campaign promise to bring the U.S. troops home, despite the deadlocked peace talks. In July 1969, the much-anticipated American withdrawal from Vietnam finally began as eight hundred soldiers from the U.S. Army's Ninth Infantry Division left for home.

WASTED LIVES

Although the phased withdrawal of U.S. troops had begun, American soldiers in South Vietnam were still heavily involved in daily combat. Yet despite the many casualties U.S. troops suffered as a result of combat operations, peace seemed no closer. One event in particular came to symbolize the futility of the ongoing American war effort. At a site near Hue known to the Americans as Hamburger Hill, forty-six men of the 101st Airborne Division were killed and four hundred wounded during a fierce ten-day battle against North Vietnamese troops. After finally capturing the hill, however, the Americans were inexplicably told by their commander the next day to abandon it. North Vietnamese forces then moved in and took the hill back completely unopposed.

The costly assault at Hamburger Hill and its aftermath provoked a firestorm of criticism back in Washington among members of Congress, who complained that American lives were being wasted in Vietnam. One senator called the Hamburger Hill battle senseless and irresponsible. To mute such criticism, U.S. military commanders in Vietnam were told by their superiors in Washington to avoid such major battles in the future. From that point on, small patrols would conduct

Richard Nixon becomes the thirty-seventh U.S. president. In his 1969 inaugural speech, Nixon pledged to get America out of the Vietnam War.

VIET CONG CONDITIONS IN 1969

In this excerpt from Portrait of the Enemy (by David Chanoff and Doan Van Toai) Viet Cong troop commander Trinh Duc comments on the conditions he faced in 1969 and his reaction to the start of the American troop withdrawal.

"There's no doubt that 1969 was the worst year we faced, at least the worst year I faced. There was no food, no future—nothing bright. But 1969 was also the time I was happiest. I destroyed several American tanks from the *Flying Horses* tank battalion that was stationed in Suoi Ram. I did it with pressure mines that our bombmakers made from unexploded American bombs. Each mine had fifteen pounds of TNT. I was given an award as a champion tank killer. The year 1969 was also the period when the true heroism of the peasants showed itself. Although we were isolated from the villagers, many of them risked their lives to get food to us. They devised all sorts of ingenious ways to get rice through the government checkpoints. Their feeling for us was one of the things that gave me courage to go on. Another thing was the conviction the Americans couldn't last. In 1969 they began to pull out some of their troops. We believed that eventually they would have to withdraw altogether. We knew that even though we faced tremendous difficulties, so did they. They had terrible problems, especially at home. We didn't think their government could stand it in the long run. That gave me heart."

search-and-destroy missions instead of larger units mounting major assaults on enemy positions.

Hamburger Hill ended any illusion among American troops that they might achieve a great military victory such as the one the United States had enjoyed in World War II. Instead, soldiers now knew they were simply holding on until some kind of peace settlement could be worked out between America's leaders and the North Vietnamese. The knowledge that no amount of personal sacrifice would change the war's outcome seriously eroded morale and made troops less inclined to engage the enemy. "Nobody wants to be the last guy to die in Vietnam,"[25] a young captain on his first tour of duty in Vietnam aptly commented.

Vietnam had thus become an unpopular war in which the main task of the common soldier was to stay alive while counting down the days until the year-long tour of combat duty typically required of American soldiers was up. Retired general Norman Schwarzkopf, who commanded a battalion in Vietnam during this tumultuous period, recalls, "It didn't take the troops very long to figure out on night ambushes that if they didn't shoot at the enemy, the enemy wouldn't shoot at them."[26]

Schwarzkopf also blamed the ineffectiveness of American troops in the field on the lack of support for the war among the American public:

> We had no professional leadership, and the troops knew what was going on [the antiwar protests] back in the States. They were drafted and sent over to a war that wasn't being supported by the American people. I don't blame them. If I was a private drafted and knew that all these other guys back home were getting off and I wasn't, I don't think I would have been a very good fighter either.[27]

A HATED WAR

The war's unpopularity among both American soldiers and civilians back home was clear to the North Vietnamese, who keenly watched news reports that contained footage of antiwar demonstrations in America. The North Vietnamese even went so far as to openly support American antiwar protesters. Prior to a planned nationwide demonstration against the war known as the Moratorium, North Vietnam's prime minister, Pham Van Dong, broadcast a message of support to protest participants, saying, "May your fall offensive succeed splendidly."[28]

Such overt efforts by the North Vietnamese to sway public opinion in the United States did little to change official American policies. In fact, conservative politicians in the United States were infuriated by the thought that Communists from North Vietnam were encouraging the American antiwar movement. President Nixon addressed the issue during a TV speech, stating that internal divisions were harmful to American interests: "the more divided we are at home, the less likely the enemy is to negotiate at Paris. . . . North Vietnam cannot defeat or humiliate the United States. Only Americans can do that."[29] But events in Vietnam and the United States would soon leave Americans more divided than ever.

Throughout South Vietnam, the Communists began a new offensive, attacking more than 150 targets. In response, Nixon ordered aerial bombing raids against the Ho Chi Minh Trail. Nixon also ordered the bombing of North Vietnamese supply bases located inside Cambodia, although these missions were carried out in secret since Cambodia was officially neutral. Nixon also was aware that NVA troops had been massing just over the border, so he became convinced that further action was needed in Cambodia. To break up this troop concentration and to weaken the overall strength of the North Vietnamese forces as a prelude to the U.S. departure from Vietnam, in May 1970 Nixon ordered U.S. and South Vietnamese ground troops into Cambodia.

To explain this invasion of neutral Cambodia to the American people, the president once again went on TV and said the attack was "not for the purpose of expanding the war into Cambodia but for the purpose of ending the war in Vietnam and winning the just peace we desire."[30] Despite Nixon's contention that

Antiwar activists protest the Vietnam War and Nixon's call for the invasion of Cambodia.

his actions were not designed to widen the war, the Cambodian incursion generated a tidal wave of protests from U.S. politicians, the press, college students, professors, clergy members, business leaders, and many average Americans.

VIETNAMIZATION

By December 1971, U.S. troop levels had dropped to just 156,800 from a peak of 543,400. To get all American forces out of Vietnam as he had repeatedly promised, Nixon and his advisers had come up with a strategy that they called "Vietnamization." What Nixon envisioned was that South Vietnamese troops would gradually take over all of the fighting as the Americans departed. As part of this plan, the Army of the Republic of Vietnam (ARVN), entirely equipped and supplied by the United States, was being rapidly increased to a million soldiers.

To operate this huge army, South Vietnamese officers and technicians were given crash courses in everything from how to repair helicopters to lessons on large-scale battle tactics. The South Vietnamese had much to learn, since up to this point the ARVN commanders had depended entirely on American senior officers in Saigon for advice on the day-to-day conduct of the war. U.S. admiral Robert Salzer, who observed the situation, said the South Vietnamese were being asked "to undertake a superhuman task of absorbing the full load of military

TROOPS BORDERING ON DISASTER

Many Americans were surprisingly unaware that conditions had seriously deteriorated in the U.S. military as a result of the Vietnam quagmire. In 1971, Colonel Robert D. Heinl, a twenty-seven-year marine veteran, wrote an article for Armed Forces Journal *titled "The Collapse of the Armed Forces" that drew national attention for its blunt assessment of the problems plaguing America's troops. The following, which appeared in John Clark Pratt's* Vietnam Voices: Perspectives on the War Years 1941–1982, *is an excerpt of that article.*

"The morale, discipline and battle-worthiness of the U.S. Armed Forces are, with a few salient exceptions, lower and worse than at any time in this century and possibly in the history of the United States. By every conceivable indicator, our army that now remains in Vietnam is in a state approaching collapse, with individual units avoiding or having refused combat, murdering their officers and non-commissioned officers, drug-ridden, and dispirited where not near-mutinous. . . . It is in Vietnam that the rearguard of a 500,000-man army, in its day. . . the best army the United States ever put into the field, is numbly extricating itself from a nightmare war the Armed Forces feel they had foisted on them by bright civilians [in the White House] who are now back on campus writing books about the folly of it all. . . . Admiral Elmo R. Zumwalt, Chief of Naval Operations, minces no words. 'We have a personnel crisis,' he recently said, 'that borders on disaster.'"

An exhausted American soldier naps. Exhaustion added to the low morale felt by armed forces as the war progressed.

defense with sophisticated equipment . . . in far too short a time."[31]

The South Vietnamese were soon put to the test. Beginning in March 1972, things took a turn for the worse in Vietnam as some 200,000 North Vietnamese soldiers, commanded by General Vo Nguyen Giap, began an all-out attempt to crush South Vietnam's army and win the war. This so-called Easter Offensive resulted in some of the heaviest fighting of the entire war. By this time, most of the American ground troops had gone home and South Vietnam's troops bore the brunt of the attack. To aid the South Vietnamese, President Nixon authorized a massive bombing campaign by American pilots against the invading troops. He also approved the dropping of mines into North Vietnam's harbors and intensified the bombing of roads, bridges, and oil facilities in North Vietnam.

The American bombing campaign tipped the balance in favor of South Vietnam's army. An estimated 100,000 North Vietnamese soldiers and some 40,000 South Vietnamese troops died during the offensive. North Vietnam's goal of conquering the south outright had been thwarted, giving Nixon hope that he could now bring the war to a negotiated end.

PEACE IS AT HAND

For three years, the Paris peace talks had been completely bogged down. Now, America's domestic politics came into play. Nixon was up for reelection in 1972. Although he was leading in the polls and appeared well on the way toward winning reelection, Nixon was anxious to assure victory at the polls by securing some

kind of peace settlement. To break the deadlocked peace talks, Nixon had sent foreign policy expert Henry Kissinger to conduct secret negotiations with the North Vietnamese. In October, a month before the election, the stalemate in Paris finally ended as the United States and North Vietnam both agreed to major concessions. North Vietnam dropped its long-standing demand for the removal of South Vietnam's anti-Communist government. The United States, for its part, agreed to allow North Vietnamese troops already positioned inside South Vietnam to remain there indefinitely. On election day, November 7, 1972, Richard Nixon was voted a second term as president in the biggest landslide to date in U.S. history.

Nixon and the American people were jubilant over the pending peace treaty, but in reality there were still some big obstacles to overcome. For one thing, South Vietnam's president, Nguyen Van Thieu, strongly opposed the treaty. In all, Thieu proposed sixty-nine amendments to the peace treaty, but perhaps his greatest objection was to the provision that allowed North Vietnamese troops to remain in South Vietnam. The United States attempted to appease Thieu by giving serious consideration to his list of amendments. The North Vietnamese responded to this new development by walking out of the peace talks altogether. Once again, the peace process had become deadlocked.

A furious Nixon issued an ultimatum to the North Vietnamese, demanding they return to the peace talks within seventy-two hours or face renewed bombing. When the North Vietnamese ignored his warning, Nixon ordered eleven days of

*Representatives from the United States (left) and North Vietnam (right)
meet to discuss concessions at the Paris peace talks in 1968.*

maximum-force air strikes against military targets in North Vietnam. The bombings were denounced worldwide by national leaders, news commentators, and religious figures, including the pope. Still, the bombing went on, until on December 26, 1972, the North Vietnamese agreed to return to the negotiations.

Over the next few weeks, all remaining differences were resolved between the United States and North Vietnam. The Paris Peace Accords, which concluded America's involvement in the Vietnam War, were signed on January 27, 1973. Under the treaty's terms, the United States agreed to withdraw all of its re-

maining troops from Vietnam within sixty days. The North Vietnamese agreed to an immediate cease-fire and the release of 591 American prisoners of war. An estimated 150,000 North Vietnamese soldiers inside South Vietnam were allowed to remain in place.

Under intense pressure from President Nixon, who had threatened to cut off all American aid if he balked, South Vietnam's president Thieu reluctantly went along with the peace treaty. Thieu considered the provision allowing North Vietnamese forces to stay in his country "tantamount to surrender."[32] But along with his threats, Nixon had also reassured

Thieu by promising that America would "take swift and severe retaliatory action"[33] should North Vietnam violate the peace agreement.

On March 29, 1973, the last remaining American troops withdrew from Vietnam as President Nixon declared, "The day we have all worked and prayed for has finally come."[34] America's longest war, and its first defeat, had thus concluded. During twelve years of warfare, 2.9 million American men and women had served in Vietnam, with half a million seeing actual combat. There were 47,382 Americans killed in action, and 10,811 died in noncombat situations. Another 153,303 were wounded, 74,000 survived as quadriplegics or multiple amputees.

THE ENDURING LEGACY

For the Vietnamese, the enduring legacy of America's involvement in their long struggle was the incredible destruction caused by aerial bombing. From 1965 to 1972, U.S. jets dropped nearly 8 million tons of bombs in Vietnam, four times the tonnage used during all of World War II. Ironically, most of the bombs had not been dropped in North Vietnam but in South Vietnam, against Viet Cong and North Vietnamese troop positions. The bombs, however, devastated Vietnam's rural civilian population as well, killing many thousands and leaving nearly 3 million homeless.

Reacting to the war's bitter legacy, legislators sought to make certain that no

AN UNWINNABLE WAR

In a 2001 Time magazine article, American historian Stanley Karnow, who won a Pulitzer Prize for writing what many consider to be the definitive history of the Vietnam War, commented on U.S. ignorance regarding Vietnam and the overwhelming desire of the North Vietnamese to win.

"We trickled into Vietnam with no knowledge of the country or its culture. Worse, we were oblivious to its people. Lean, sinewy figures in rubber sandals, black cotton pajamas and conic basket hats, we dismissed them as 'primitive.' But they were a highly sophisticated folk whose civilization dated back millenniums. Over those centuries they recurrently resisted foreign invaders, particularly their predatory Chinese neighbors. That tumultuous history ingrained in them an intensely nationalistic spirit illustrated by their willingness to give their lives for their cause. . . . I asked [North Vietnam's former commander, General Giap] during an interview in Hanoi in 1990 how long he would have gone on fighting against the U.S. He thundered, 'Another 20, maybe 100 years, as long as it took to win, regardless of cost.' We faced an enemy that, like bamboo, could be bent but not broken. As a result, the war was essentially unwinnable."

future American president would send troops into combat without first receiving permission from Congress. On June 19, 1973, Congress forbade any further U.S. military actions in Vietnam and all of Southeast Asia. From then on, there would be no more U.S. bombings in Vietnam or Cambodia. Congress further clamped down in November 1973 by passing the War Powers Resolution, requiring the president to obtain the approval of Congress within ninety days of sending U.S. troops into combat overseas, and to report to Congress within forty-eight hours of ordering such combat.

THE SOUTH'S TROUBLED ARMY

The actions by the U.S. Congress meant that the burden of preventing a victory by North Vietnam rested entirely on South Vietnam's army. Although the Army of the Republic of Vietnam had been in existence since the early 1960s, this force had always depended heavily on aid from the United States. All of the military matériel used by ARVN troops, from helicopters to cannons and rifles, to the uniforms on their backs, came from America.

Now, in addition to effectively precluding direct American involvement in Vietnam, Congress began questioning the spending of billions of U.S. taxpayer dollars to support an army that American military figures admitted was only achieving mixed results. In fact, throughout the war, many American commanders in Vietnam had doubted ARVN's combat effectiveness and questioned the willingness of South Vietnamese soldiers to fight. Veteran John Kerry later recalled, "There were too many times that I went

out on missions with Vietnamese soldiers only to discover they disappeared when the going got rough."[35] Another Vietnam veteran was equally blunt in his assessment of the ARVN forces: "The ARVN as a force was undependable. . . . The essential ingredient [was] missing, and that's dedication and will and enthusiasm. I don't think it was instilled in the ARVN."[36]

Most American observers agreed that corruption and incompetence had plagued South Vietnam's army from the start. High-ranking ARVN officers were promoted because of their political loyalty to South Vietnam's president, not because of their military prowess. These political appointees lacked the competence that would have earned them the respect of those they commanded. One American general remarked, "Only a handful of [ARVN] generals had the confidence of lower-ranking officers, who in turn felt that the generals were more concerned with their own personal welfare than that of the country."[37] These senior officers, knowing how little stock their men placed in their decisions, often chose to quickly pull back when the enemy attacked in order to avoid casualties.

In addition to poor leadership, corruption hampered the ARVN's efforts. Some high-ranking ARVN officers had gotten rich by diverting U.S. aid for their own benefit. Huge ships arrived in South Vietnam each week, carrying everything from home appliances to tanks to farm equipment. These shipments were intended to bolster South Vietnam's war effort by strengthening the nation's economy, but up to 40 percent of the goods sent to Vietnam were stolen and wound up being sold on the thriving black market.

South Vietnamese troops return from a training exercise. Inexperience and lack of equipment doomed the South's campaign against the North.

So corrupt were some officers that military equipment destined for South Vietnam's army was sometimes even sold to the Viet Cong.

By 1974, Congress and the American people had grown utterly weary of anything to do with Vietnam. Noting the desire of most Americans to leave the whole tumultuous legacy of their nation's involvement in Vietnam behind, in September 1974, Congress voted to cut back aid to South Vietnam to just $700 million for 1975, leaving South Vietnam's army without adequate supplies. Furthermore, the nation lacked the wherewithal to pur-

chase war matériel from other sources. As a result, morale and military readiness, already shaky, plunged even further among South Vietnam's troops. Twenty-five years later, retired general Norman Schwarzkopf recalled the funding cuts and blamed them for the disaster that befell South Vietnam:

> What lost the war for us—after we turned over our helicopters, artillery, and sophisticated equipment to the [South] Vietnamese—was Congress cutting off the money. That cut off the supply of critical spare parts and am-

munition that the South Vietnamese needed to employ what we had left behind for them. That was it. The war was over. That was an act of betrayal, an absolute act of betrayal. . . . It was one of the blackest moments in the history of the United States of America, because the day that happened, the South Vietnamese were doomed. China and Russia were still supporting North Vietnam, but we betrayed the South after giving them our word.[38]

North Vietnam's top military commanders closely observed the ongoing situation in South Vietnam and concluded that the south's troops were growing weaker every day. Certainly from a logis-

tical standpoint, that assessment was correct. Thirty-five percent of South Vietnam's tanks and half of its armored personnel carriers had become inoperative due to a lack of spare parts. Supplies of tires, batteries, rifle barrels, and fuel also plummeted to critically low levels.

In stark contrast to the dismal condition of South Vietnam's army, North Vietnam's army, fully equipped with weapons supplied by China and the Soviet Union, had never been stronger. For North Vietnam's leaders, the question was not whether but when to undertake the conquest of the south. By the beginning of 1975, they had a plan for that takeover worked out; South Vietnam's days were literally numbered.

3 South Vietnam Collapses

As North Vietnam's leaders contemplated an invasion of South Vietnam, they faced one uncertainty: Richard Nixon was no longer U.S. president, and they had no idea how his successor, Gerald R. Ford, would react. To test Ford's resolve, in December 1974, two NVA divisions attacked and easily overran a lightly defended outpost in South Vietnam's Phuoc Long province. President Ford responded to this clear violation of the Paris Peace Accords with a diplomatic protest, but in accordance with the congressional ban on all U.S. military activity in Southeast Asia, he ordered no armed intervention. Former North Vietnamese general Tran Con Man later recalled,

> The Phuoc Long attack was a carefully calculated experiment. We wanted to test the American and the South Vietnamese governments. . . . And, of course, there was no response. That was what we wanted to find out— would they respond or were they ready to let go? They were ready to let go.[39]

Within days of the attack on Phuoc Long, North Vietnam's senior military and political leaders met in Hanoi to form a battle plan for final victory. On January 8, 1975, they approved an invasion that involved twenty NVA divisions.

A few weeks after that fateful meeting, North Vietnam's belief that America would not intervene was confirmed when President Ford bluntly stated during a press conference that the United States was unwilling to reinvolve itself militarily in Vietnam. After hearing this statement, North Vietnam's first secretary, Le Duan, told his comrades, "Never have we had military and political conditions so perfect or a strategic advantage so great as we have now."[40]

In preparation for the attack, massive amounts of NVA weaponry rolled into South Vietnam along the Ho Chi Minh Trail. By now, portions of the old jungle trail had been transformed into smooth highways made of crushed limestone and gravel. A journey along the trail that had once taken up to four months now took a mere ten days. At any one time, as many as ten thousand trucks, loaded with military gear, were moving along the trail in broad daylight. With South Vietnam's air force hampered by shortages of ammunition and working aircraft, North Vietnam could send all the weaponry it needed south without fear of attack. The trucks, along with tanks, troops, and artillery, were all strategically positioned, ready for attack.

THE FINAL OFFENSIVE

North Vietnam began its all-out offensive against South Vietnam at 2:00 A.M. on March 10, 1975, as twenty-five thousand Communist troops attacked the city of Ban Me Thuot in the Central Highlands region. The attack took the four thousand South Vietnamese positioned there by surprise, and many soldiers quickly surrendered to the Communists. Others deserted their posts and dashed off to help get their families to safety. It was com-

President Gerald Ford protested NVA incursions in South Vietnam but did nothing more.

mon practice in South Vietnam for soldiers to bring their families with them to wherever they were stationed. Upon being attacked, the soldiers' first worry was the well-being of their nearby families, and this phenomenon would be observed repeatedly in the coming weeks.

Following the overnight collapse of the defenses at Ban Me Thuot, South Vietnam's president Nguyen Van Thieu made a strategic decision to withdraw his forces from the entire Central Highlands region, along with two northern provinces. The equivalent of three whole divisions of South Vietnamese soldiers vacating their posts without firing a shot dumbfounded the North Vietnamese and left them suspicious of South Vietnam's intentions, as former NVA general Tran Con Man recalled:

> We had expected a very intense and long battle with the South around Ban Me Thuot. But the way Mr. Thieu responded to the attack was not even within our imagination. In fact, his response created a great question in our minds as to whether or not this was a trap, a brilliant tactic to lure us in. . . . Therefore our commanders moved ahead very cautiously at first, looking for the trap. . . . We thought the South was planning some big surprise. But when Thieu [also] withdrew his troops from [the strategic town of]

A DYSFUNCTIONAL ARMY

During North Vietnam's final offensive, South Vietnam's army (ARVN) had become utterly dysfunctional and was ripe for defeat, as former South Vietnamese general Ly Tong Ba recalled in Tears Before the Rain: An Oral History of the Fall of South Vietnam *(by Larry Engelmann).*

"The soldiers of the ARVN in the end believed that they had been lied to. Look, they were in a bad situation. . . . The Americans were not helping them any more and their own government was not helping them, either. They were fighting and dying, and for what? Some of my soldiers finally started to run. . . . And when I saw that, I could not do anything else. The [U.S.] Army was finally gone. . . . The society of [South] Vietnam had become corrupted and chaotic, and that kind of attitude got into the [South] Vietnamese army and soldiers, too. The commanders' mentality was not a fighting mentality. When the fight became tough, they didn't want to fight any more. They wanted to depend on America, and when they could not depend on America they ran away. That was the sickness that they had caught. . . . The Northern soldiers overran all of our positions. . . . So when the enemy told us to lay down our weapons, many men just put down their weapons."

Pleiku, we realized suddenly that there was no trap, and there was no plan, and the South was not up to fighting anymore. That is when we decided to chase them as fast as we could.[41]

Thieu's original idea was to regroup his forces farther south around Saigon, where they would make a final stand. However, the sight of so many of their comrades withdrawing from the highlands ignited a panicked retreat of still more South Vietnamese troops. Civilians from the area, witnessing what appeared to be a full-blown military retreat, joined the soldiers heading south. This disorga-

nized mass of people, numbering nearly 200,000, meandered along an old logging road at a snail's pace. As the throngs fled, they were ruthlessly bombarded by the NVA. The retreat came to be known as the Convoy of Tears as thousands of people, civilians and soldiers alike, died from the shelling. Others perished from lack of food and water or from sheer exhaustion.

The unchallenged advance of North Vietnam's forces generated an ever-increasing tidal wave of panicked humanity. The flood of refugees and soldiers swelled still further as more and more soldiers simply dropped their weapons and joined in the chaotic retreat along with their families. To observers, it seemed as if all of South Vietnam was on the move. Some ARVN units did attempt to stand and fight, but their efforts were hampered by critical shortages, as South Vietnamese colonel Cau Le later recalled:

> We didn't have enough ammunition and supplies to fight big battles. We could only fire five artillery rounds a day for each gun. There was a limited gas supply for my trucks. We had a shortage of batteries for radio communications and parts for tanks. When we made heavy contact with the enemy, we severely lacked fire [power] and other support, which reduced our ability to fight considerably.[42]

To North Vietnam's leaders, the ease with which the whole offensive was proceeding was absolutely astounding. The plan had called for a more gradual takeover of the south, but sensing the chance for a total victory years ahead of schedule, North Vietnam's senior leaders met and decided to push on to victory, declaring, "A new strategic opportunity has come, and conditions allow [for] an

An injured child clings to her mother as she and thousands of other civilians flee NVA shelling in a retreat known as the Convoy of Tears.

Running Again: The Last Retreat

Writer Philip Caputo penned this on-the-scene report, first published in the Chicago Tribune *on April 28, 1975, as he watched a gigantic column of South Vietnamese civilians head for Saigon, fleeing the North Vietnamese advance. It is excerpted from* Reporting Vietnam, vol. 2, American Journalism, 1969–1975.

"What is happening here is an exodus of humanity of staggering magnitude, so staggering that no words of mine can capture anything but the smallest fraction of it. . . . A hundred yards away, North Vietnamese mortar shells and rockets are slamming into government positions guarding the bridge over the Dong Hai River, whose brown waters meander with mocking indifference through green rice fields and murky swamps. . . . Pouring over the river bridge is another kind of stream, a stream of flesh and blood and bone, of exhausted, frightened faces, of crushed hopes and loss. The long, relentless column reaches forward and backward as far as the eye can see, for miles and miles and in places 50 feet across. . . . They are filing past me on foot, their sandals scraping mournfully against the pavement, their heads hunched down against the driving monsoon rain that lashes them. They are riding on motor scooters, in cars, in trucks, buses, oxcarts all piled up with crates and suitcases and ragged bundles of clothes. Sometimes the noise of the vehicles is deafening, but not so deafening as to drown out the wind-rushing sound of an incoming rocket that whips over their heads to burst in the paddylands beyond the river. At other times, all you hear is that solemn, processional shuffling of sandaled feet, bare feet, bloodied feet against the rainslick asphalt. You hear that and the chorusing of crying children."

early completion of our resolution to liberate the South. We resolve to rapidly concentrate our forces, weapons and material to liberate Saigon before the rainy season."[43]

As the North Vietnamese offensive continued to gain momentum, ARVN senior officers abandoned their commands in order to be with their families. Meanwhile, South Vietnam's president Thieu was plagued with indecision over how to use the remaining troops at his disposal. Incredibly, formal plans to regroup South Vietnam's forces for a defense of Saigon had never actually been drawn up. As a result, no real defense was mounted. Even top ARVN commanders profess puzzlement over what befell their country. One former South Vietnamese general recalled, "I know that we had the forces to form a front somewhere. But nothing happened. They never turned around and fought. I don't know what happened."[44]

Thieu's continuing indecision and a deepening confusion and panic among the south's highest-ranking military commanders allowed motorized columns of North Vietnamese to roll unopposed throughout South Vietnam. A former NVA general recalled, "Night and day our troops roared forward, advancing at lightning speed, in high spirits and confident of victory."[45] A European journalist on the scene marveled at how the north's forces were advancing in a way unprecedented in their long struggle:

> For thirty years they [the Communists] had been fighting an exhausting guerrilla campaign involving tremendous sacrifices and physical hardships. Now, suddenly, they were discovering the exhilaration of a mobile war, the thrill of advancing on the enemy in a victorious sweep, carrying all before them. The barefoot guerrilla bands had been transformed into a Russian-style armor-plated juggernaut.[46]

A HOUSE OF CARDS

After taking the entire Central Highlands region, the NVA juggernaut set its sights on the historic city of Hue, located near the coast. As the Communist forces approached the city, South Vietnamese officers and soldiers positioned there made a hasty retreat by sea south toward the city of Da Nang. Panicked by being left defenseless, and remembering the Communist massacres during the 1968 Tet Offensive of those who supported the south's regime, a million of the city's civilian residents fled as well. On March 25, Hue fell without resistance to the North Vietnamese.

The next objective for the NVA was Da Nang itself, South Vietnam's second largest city. In Da Nang, wild rumors spread that South Vietnam's leaders had already decided to abandon the city to the Communists. In a panic, nearly 3 million of the city's civilian residents attempted to flee southward all at once, completely jamming all exit routes. At the city's harbor, an orderly boat evacuation quickly became a nightmare as refugees stormed the docks trying to board barges that had been brought there to move soldiers south to defend Saigon. Civilians and soldiers also stormed Da Nang's airport, and any incoming aircraft was mobbed the moment it landed by people desperate to board. Jan Wollett, a flight attendant on the very last passenger jet out of Da Nang, recalled how the panic brought out murderous impulses in some:

> When we landed it was very strange, because we did not see a soul at first. Nobody. The entire airfield was deserted. And then, as we started to taxi, a massive swarm of people came up and out of the bunkers. Thousands—and I mean literally thousands—started racing toward us. They were running, they were on motorcycles, they were in vans, they were in jeeps and cars and personnel

South Vietnamese soldiers fill all available space on a ship escaping the NVA.

eyed. . . . A family of five was running a few feet from me, reaching out for help to get on board. . . . I reached back to grab the mother's hand, but before I could get it, a man running behind them shot all five of them, and they fell and were trampled by the crowd. . . . And the man who shot them stepped on them to get closer to the air stair . . . and ran up into the aircraft.[47]

Inside Da Nang, the South Vietnamese military commanders had fled, leaving 100,000 of their soldiers to face the invaders on their own. Surrounded by NVA troops, they surrendered on March 30, after holding out for just thirty-two hours. Proof of how utterly demoralized these ARVN forces were is that the North Vietnamese force numbered only thirty-five thousand, barely a third of the south's troop strength.

After Da Nang fell, one city after another surrendered to the Communists without a struggle. By early April, more than half of South Vietnam had been conquered by the North Vietnamese, causing an ever-increasing number of panicked South Vietnamese soldiers and civilians to flee toward Saigon, South Vietnam's

carriers, they were on bicycles—they were coming out to us in anything they could find. . . . Then the soldiers started coming on board. They were running. And they were just wild-

capital. People grabbed any possible means of transport they could find, including bicycles and motorbikes, or they hitched a ride on any passing vehicle. Along the roadside, those less able to fend for themselves got trampled or even run over by fast-moving South Vietnamese military vehicles roaring southward in full retreat.

By now, the North Vietnamese were ready to begin their final push toward Saigon in what they called the Ho Chi Minh Campaign in honor of the late leader, who had died of old age in 1969. Only at the town of Xuan Loc, thirty-eight miles northeast of Saigon, did the North Vietnamese encounter sustained resistance from South Vietnamese troops.

"FLEEING IN THEIR SHORTS!"

South Vietnam's final collapse on April 30, 1975, assumed a tragicomic aspect, as revealed in this excerpt from a Time *magazine article by George J. Church, written on the twentieth anniversary of the fall of South Vietnam.*

"South Vietnamese soldiers confronting NVA columns entering Saigon on April 30 did not just flee; they threw away everything that could identify them as soldiers and tried to melt into the general population. Bui Tin, an NVA colonel and journalist, said he spent that last morning 'with one of our units taking a fortress that had been held by a South Vietnamese division. All the South Vietnamese soldiers who had fled had abandoned their uniforms. Everywhere you looked on the road, they had left all their military clothing and supplies: canteens, caps, coats, pants, boots, belts—they must have ended up fleeing in their shorts!' . . . That set the stage for the final, and almost comically unheroic, scene of the war. NVA Major Nguyen Van Hoa, commanding tank No. 843, a Soviet-made T-54, with six other tanks following, had entered Saigon before dawn. His little column ran into a brief firefight at the Thi Nghe bridge, knocking out two ARVN M41 tanks. Rolling into almost deserted streets, the column kept going toward its target, the Presidential Palace. But where was it? Says Major Hoa: 'The only directions we had were to go through seven intersections and we would find the palace.' His column split up; at the head of three tanks, 843 clattered down a boulevard so lined with leafy trees that 'we couldn't see what was at the end. We met a woman on a motorcycle, and we stopped to ask her where the palace was. It was right there.'"

North Vietnamese simply bypassed Xuan Loc and headed for the city of Bien Hoa, which was closer still to Saigon. By April 16, defenders at both Xuan Loc and Bien Hoa had run low on ammunition and resistance withered. For North Vietnam's army, the road to Saigon now lay wide open.

A HOPELESS SITUATION

As their defenses crumbled, South Vietnam's president Thieu and the nation's top military leaders remained convinced that the United States would come to their rescue. Thieu's reasoning was based on U.S. president Richard Nixon's personal assurance, made years earlier, that the United States would "take swift and retaliatory action"[48] if South Vietnam's survival was ever threatened. But now, whatever Nixon's intentions might have been, he was long gone and Nixon's successor had no intention of direct intervention.

South Vietnamese president Nguyen Van Thieu meets with U.S. military officials in 1967. The hoped for rescue at war's end never came.

There, for two weeks, members of South Vietnam's Eighteenth Army Division stubbornly held out. By this time, however, such resistance was irrelevant. The

President Ford did request emergency military aid for South Vietnam. But members of Congress had no desire to approve any funds that would prolong the fighting in Vietnam. Influential senator Mike Mansfield bluntly stated that he was "sick and tired of pictures of [Southeast Asian] men, women, and children being slaughtered by American guns with American ammunition in countries in which we have no vital interest."[49] Fellow senator Hubert Humphrey added that such assistance would not change the conflict's outcome, saying that more U.S. aid to South Vietnam would "merely prolong the agony."[50]

With the Communists seemingly on the verge of victory, several South Vietnamese generals decided to attempt to arrange a last-minute compromise that would preserve some degree of independence for a shrunken South Vietnam. Knowing that it was unlikely the Communists would ever negotiate with such a staunch anti-Communist as President Thieu, the generals, with the blessing of the U.S. ambassador to South Vietnam, Graham Martin, pressured Thieu to resign.

On Monday, April 21, President Thieu appeared on Vietnamese television and delivered a rambling ninety-minute resignation speech. During the speech, he read from the letter Nixon had sent him back in 1972 promising military action if South Vietnam was ever threatened. Thieu tearfully condemned the Paris Peace Accords, Henry Kissinger, and America itself: "The United States has not respected its promises. It is inhumane. It is untrustworthy. It is irresponsible."[51]

Two days later, in a speech at Tulane University, President Ford made it clear that he was unmoved by Thieu's words. The Vietnam conflict, Ford said, was "a war that is finished as far as America is concerned."[52] In fact, the war was nearing its end. As Ford spoke, more than 100,000 North Vietnamese soldiers were advancing toward Saigon itself. Inside the city, some thirty thousand South Vietnamese

soldiers waited, but they had been abandoned by their commanders, who themselves were trying to flee the country by either air or sea.

THE FALL OF SAIGON

Until now, Saigon had remained eerily calm despite the influx of refugees and the obvious wholesale collapse of South Vietnam's army. A journalist on the scene later recalled, "The coffee shops and restaurants [in Saigon] were all open and the city dwellers carried on with their business as if everything was normal."[53] Meanwhile, an orderly round-the-clock evacuation of U.S. personnel and South Vietnamese civilians who had worked closely with the Americans was already under way at Tan Son Nhut air base, which served as Saigon's main airport. Saigon's fragile calm was soon shattered, however, as NVA troops fired four heavy rockets into the downtown area, killing ten people, wounding over two hundred, and sparking a huge fire that destroyed the homes of five thousand people. South Vietnam's new president, General Duong Van Minh, appealed for a cease-fire. But the North Vietnamese ignored his appeal and instead shelled the runways at Tan Son Nhut, putting them out of service.

Realizing the end was fast approaching, President Ford ordered an emergency helicopter evacuation of some seven thousand remaining Americans and South Vietnamese allies from Saigon. As a prearranged signal to those who were slated for evacuation, the song "White Christmas" was broadcast over U.S.

THE HUMAN COST

On Wednesday morning, April 30, 1975, Saigon finally fell. Hai Van Le, of South Vietnam's air force, is quoted in Larry Engelmann's *Tears Before the Rain: An Oral History of the Fall of South Vietnam* as saying, "It was a very nice day. The sun was shining. And everyone was crying." General Van Tien Dung, commander of the north's final offensive, had a different perspective. In *The Vietnam Experience: The Aftermath*, by Edward Doyle et al., Dung is quoted as recalling, "Our generation had known many victorious mornings but there had been no morning so fresh and beautiful, so radiant, so clear and cool, so sweet-scented as this morning of total victory."

For both North and South Vietnam, the cost of the war in human terms had been staggering. South Vietnam counted up to 250,000 soldiers killed in action and almost 500,000 wounded. South Vietnamese civilians fared worse than their military. Up to 400,000 civilians were killed and an estimated 1 million wounded. Fighting for North Vietnam, the Viet Cong and North Vietnamese Army counted up to 900,000 killed, and 65,000 North Vietnamese civilians are estimated to have died.

U.S. Marines evacuate Vietnamese civilians following the fall of Saigon.

Armed Forces Radio. On the morning of April 29, after the shelling had subsided at Tan Son Nhut, U.S. helicopters arrived and succeeded in evacuating nearly 4,500 Vietnamese and 395 U.S. civilians. The evacuation then shifted to the American embassy compound several miles away, where thousands of South Vietnamese slated for evacuation, unable to get to Tan Son Nhut, were stranded along with remaining Americans, journalists, and other foreigners. A detachment of U.S. Marines in full combat gear arrived by helicopter to secure the facility. But the situation deteriorated when a growing throng of South Vietnamese civilians frantically attempted to get inside the compound by climbing over the high walls. Marine major Jim Kean remembered the evacuation:

> By the afternoon of the twenty-ninth, my guess was that we had as many as ten thousand people outside the Embassy, and perhaps 160 Marine guards to secure the perimeter. There were not enough Marines to man those walls and to keep people from climbing over into the Embassy.[54]

Standing by off the coast of Vietnam were three U.S. aircraft carriers to take evacuees arriving by helicopter. Many South Vietnamese piloting ARVN helicopters also landed on the carrier decks uninvited, in many cases bringing their families along.

At this late stage in the war, the North Vietnamese wanted to avoid any incident that might provoke an American military response, so they briefly delayed their entry into Saigon proper to allow the last Americans to depart safely. But the delay was not long enough for the Americans to evacuate thousands of South Vietnamese allies who had spent years working for them. Most of these people would be at serious risk of retribution when the Communists took over, and they desperately wanted to exit the country. However, amid the rushed evacuation, they wound up being left behind to face an uncertain future under Communist rule.

The new rulers of South Vietnam arrived on the morning of April 30, 1975, roaring into Saigon in motorized columns and encountering no resistance. The mood of Saigon's residents was oddly ambivalent, as one South Vietnamese civilian who was there recalls:

> When we saw the first Communist troops—the creatures we had feared as if they were wild animals—we were struck by how ridiculously young they were. They seemed no more than children. Some of us instinctively offered them food, as if they were our kith and kin, which they were. Our conquerors marched in like long lost sons.[55]

Around noontime, North Vietnamese soldiers driving their Soviet-built T-54 tanks smashed through the gates of the presidential palace in Saigon. A lone Communist soldier ran up the steps to the presidential balcony, waving the red and blue Viet Cong flag for everyone to see. Inside the palace, President Minh was taken prisoner by the North Vietnamese and said, "I have been waiting since early this morning to transfer power to you."[56] North Vietnamese colonel Bui Tin's now-famous response was "Your power has crumbled. You have nothing in your hands to surrender and so you cannot surrender what you do not possess."[57] As instructed, Minh broadcast a radio message of unconditional surrender to whatever was left of South Vietnam's armed forces. The long ordeal of the Vietnam War had finally ended. A new era of Communist rule had begun.

4 The Communists Take Over

In the days following the Communist victory, an awkward peace descended on southern Vietnam. Conquest of the south had come so quickly that the Communists were not ready to administer the newly unified nation. At first, Communist soldiers went out of their way to reassure the populace that there would be no persecution or mass executions that many had long feared. Soldiers with loudspeakers wandered the streets of Saigon announcing over and over, "Do not worry. You will be well treated."[58]

Meanwhile, in a radio announcement, the Communists declared that Saigon was to be immediately renamed Ho Chi Minh City in honor of North Vietnam's founder. More radio announcements soon followed, including an order that all homeowners must display both the blue-and-red Viet Cong flag alongside the all-red flag of North Vietnam. An additional order stated that everyone had to hang a portrait of Ho Chi Minh inside their homes. The Communists also banned prostitution and shut down dance halls. A vaguely phrased order prohibited any kind of behavior that involved "acting like Americans."[59]

After this first flurry of announcements, a quiet period ensued as the Communist leadership tried to figure out what to do next. The lull provided just the right opportunity for Saigon's once-thriving street markets to spring back to life, ready to serve a whole new set of customers—the Communists themselves. Most of the soldiers from the impoverished north had never seen the kind of American and Japanese-made goods that were readily available in Saigon. One resident recalled,

> Saigon's shop windows and markets were choked with transistors, stereos, cameras, refrigerators, televisions—all the paraphernalia of a modern consumer society. Although they had been warned about these seductions, [young Communist soldiers] walked the streets with their eyes popping, buying up everything in sight, preyed on by happy merchants and streetwise children who quickly learned to exploit their simplicity.[60]

The tourist-like shopping sprees and sightseeing in newly named Ho Chi Minh City were interrupted on May 7, 1975, when thirty thousand Communists staged a rally to celebrate the city's capture and also to commemorate the twenty-first anniversary of the Viet Minh victory over the French at Dien Bien Phu.

Children smile at a street market in Saigon. The victorious Communist regime renamed Saigon, Ho Chi Minh City.

Several days later, the Communists staged an even bigger celebration of what they called Victory Day, which featured a massive military parade in Saigon, watched by half a million people. Among the spectators were most of the north's highest-ranking leaders, who had arrived specifically to attend this event.

Amid all of this hoopla, the nagging question remained as to what would happen to all of the ex-soldiers and workers who had formerly served South Vietnam's government or who had aided the Americans in some way. The answer came when the newly formed Military Management Committee, consisting of several NVA veterans charged with overseeing the whole Saigon area, issued its first decree. It stated that all men who had served in South Vietnam's army had to register and also surrender any weapons. All former soldiers were also ordered to report for rehabilitation, which they were told would involve productive labor and political study. The era of Communist reeducation had thus arrived.

REEDUCATION CAMPS

By North Vietnamese estimates, about 1.3 million people in the south had served in the fallen government or in its army and, therefore, needed reeducation. The Communist style of reeducation involved shipping people off to remote camps, confining them, and subjecting them to a program of exhausting physical labor combined with rigorous political indoctrination. The goal was to instill Communist philosophy in those not inclined to appreciate the values held by the new regime.

Communist writer Nguyen Ngoc Giao explained the basic approach:

> Re-education is a meticulous and long-range process. Management must be tight, continuous, comprehensive and specific. We must manage each person. We must manage their thoughts and actions, words and deeds, philosophy of life and ways of livelihood and travel. . . . We must closely combine management and education with interrogation.[61]

For the people of what had been South Vietnam, the process of reeducation

---

TERROR AMID THE CHAOS

After the fall of South Vietnam in April 1975, it took the Communists nearly a year to establish complete control. Meanwhile, various local authorities did as they pleased, as Truong Nhu Tang, a Communist who later escaped from Vietnam, revealed in his book A Vietcong Memoir: An Inside Account of the Vietnam War and Its Aftermath.

"With no strong central government in the South, various military, [Communist] Party, and government organs embarked on their own schemes for consolidating the conquered territories. These schemes were most evident in the wave of arbitrary arrests that scythed through the cities and villages. The army, local authorities, and security police all began sweeping up people who had somehow made it onto their respective lists. There was no code of laws governing who was to be taken, no authority to which any of these organs were responsible for their decisions, and no protection for those who were seized. . . . People were simply snatched from their homes or offices, often right off the street. No one knew why a neighbor or co-worker had been arrested or where a son or daughter had disappeared to. The Saigonese, already deeply disturbed by [the introduction of reeducation] camps, were seized by new fears. The initial hopefulness with which they had greeted the revolution (what hope there was left) was swallowed up by a frightened hostility. An ugly mood enveloped the city."

began on June 11, 1975. The first subjects of reeducation were the south's lowest-ranking ex-soldiers and former civil servants. These individuals underwent a three-day program of what the Communists called reform study. Against all expectations, the participants were allowed to go home each night. The next to be summoned for reeducation were mid-level ex-military officers. They were told to bring along ten days' worth of personal articles, such as clothing, pens, paper, and food. Following this, higher-ranking ex-officers and former government officials were instructed to report and to bring enough personal items for a thirty-day stay.

The leniency with which their lower-level counterparts had been treated gave the mid- and senior-level officers and bureaucrats hope that they would get off easily too. Reporting as ordered, approximately a quarter-million men were packed into trucks and driven off to any of 150 reeducation camps set up throughout Vietnam. In some cases, the men were transported to remote, deserted locations and told to construct their own camps from scratch. Other times, abandoned military installations left behind by the Americans were quickly converted into reeducation camps.

Families of the prisoners anxiously awaited their return after the designated ten- or thirty-day period. However, in the cases of most of the higher-ranking prisoners, months passed with no sign of their return. Worried relatives who inquired were curtly told by the Military Management Committee, "The government's communiqué said they were asked to bring food for only a month. The communiqué did not say that the re-

education period is one month."[62] In fact, for many, the reeducation process would go on for years.

Although the purpose of such camps was not to kill the inmates, death was a frequent visitor. Sometimes the prisoners were forced to get down on their hands and knees to clear away unexploded ordnance, such as mines, shells, and booby traps. Inexperienced in such dangerous and technically demanding tasks, prisoners frequently triggered deadly explosions. Death in the camps also came as the result of chronic malnutrition and diseases such as dysentery and malaria. Anyone disobeying a camp guard also risked death by torture or outright execution.

Daily life in a typical reeducation camp consisted of a dreary routine of hard manual labor eight hours a day, six days a week. Chores included removing jungle growth, putting up fences, repairing dilapidated buildings, and planting rice. In addition to the grueling work routine, prisoners were required to listen to seemingly endless political lectures extolling the virtues of communism and condemning America and the former leadership of South Vietnam. After each lecture, prisoners had to engage in lengthy discussions about the topic of the day. These sessions were closely monitored by their Communist instructors to ensure that everyone voiced acceptable opinions. Prisoners were also required to write long essays concerning the various political topics that had been discussed, as well as extensive confessions revealing everything they had done to oppose the Communists before the fall of South Vietnam. Former South Vietnamese colonel Cau Le recalled his experience as a self-professed reeducation-camp prisoner of war (POW):

The guards didn't physically torture me, but they mentally abused me. They threatened to kill me many times. They crushed my mentality and resistance through starvation and refusal to provide medicine when I was seriously sick. . . .We lacked food and clothes and were basically starved and cold in the winter. Besides punishing our bodies, they fed us Communist propaganda. We had to learn political lessons that accused the Americans as war criminals and neocolonists and proclaimed the [former South Vietnamese army as] puppets of America. The Vietnamese Communist Party, on the other hand, was praised excessively. They told us that Communism would defeat capitalism globally. Every night, each POW was told to criticize other POWs and himself. Every POW lived in a state of fear and distrust with others.[63]

Most prisoners realized they would be released only if they demonstrated a strong affinity for communism and a repentance of their old way of life. A demonstrated disgust with America was particularly desirable, they found.

A South Vietnamese prisoner, his face smeared with mud after being forced by his captors to lie for hours on wet ground, awaits transportation to a reeducation camp.

Gradually, the constant drumbeat of propaganda, combined with the privation, had an effect. As one former South Vietnamese soldier later recalled,

[The Communists] started to tell us stuff that was extremely strange and unbelievable and improbable. But as they told us the same things over and over again, I found myself starting to believe what they said. I began to feel that I myself had been a criminal for fighting in the [South Vietnamese army], as if I was guilty of some charges they drummed up and they dumped on our heads.[64]

However, many of South Vietnam's former senior army officers and ex-government officials stubbornly maintained their pride and refused to bend to their captors' will. As a result, these individuals spent more time in the camps. Of the approximately 1 million people sent to be reeducated, an estimated 200,000 served an average of three years, and another 240,000 served five years. About 60,000 were held for even longer periods.

The reeducation camps were just the first of many changes for the people of what had been South Vietnam. The Communists intended nothing less than a complete transformation of the south's society from top to bottom. No tradition or institution would be left untouched.

TIGHTENING THE REINS

To the Communists, the freewheeling culture of what had been South Vietnam was in dire need of reform. The Communists valued conformity above all and were eager to impose on the south the sort of tight control that had been a hallmark of the north for decades.

The first target of the new regime was the news media. Within days of taking over, the Communists shut down Saigon's boisterous daily newspapers and replaced them with papers that hewed to the party line. Next, bookstores were raided by Communist youth brigades and padlocked. Only books approved by Communist censors would be allowed to be published and sold. Private book collections were also seized from people's homes and sometimes burned in the street. Many of the south's well-known authors found themselves unable to get their work published.

The clampdown extended to popular culture. American-made films were banned, as were the formerly popular martial arts movies from Taiwan and other Asian countries. Movie theaters instead showed Communist propaganda films extolling the virtues of North Vietnam's revolutionary heroes and documentaries presenting an idealized vision of such things as life on a Communist collective farm. Upon entering the theater, viewers had to sit through the entire movie, no matter how bad it was, since it was forbidden to leave before the movie ended.

American pop music, which had been extremely popular, was also banned. Radio stations instead broadcast martial music and songs whose lyrics promoted the virtues of communism. This music, along with other types of propaganda, was broadcast via an extensive network of loudspeakers installed all over Saigon. The loudspeakers were also used to disseminate the latest rules and regulations imposed by the government.

Onlookers at a parade cheer the victory of the North Vietnamese. Those who did not support the new Communist regime were subject to punishment.

Those who failed to cooperate with the strict new regimen were subject, along with their entire families, to punishment. One could lose his or her job; children could be thrown out of school for a parent's offense. The pressure to conform to the new social order was intense, and people went along, even when doing so hurt those closest to them. According to one young Saigon resident,

> After April 30, when Saigon fell, people were forced to make public confessions and denounce their parents or their children or their friends. And

they did it. People didn't care what they said anymore. Everybody was simply worried about making a good impression and surviving. You had to say things in order for the new order to treat you nicely. I was saying I hated people like my parents because of what they said and what they expected from us. I wanted to survive, and I didn't care what I said. . . . Every morning at six they woke us up with two loudspeakers. . . . We went out in the street and they took roll, and we did exercises. No matter how old you

CRAVING FOOD DAY AND NIGHT

Subsisting on a starvation diet of only three hundred grams of foods, such as rice, corn, or manioc each day, many prisoners in the reeducation camps developed an overwhelming food obsession, as revealed in this anonymous letter smuggled out of one camp and reprinted in The Vietnam Experience: The Aftermath.

"In our conversation we only talk about eating and how to find things to eat. When we do not talk about eating, we silently think about eating. As soon as we finish lunch, we begin to imagine the supper awaiting us when we return from the field. The food put into the mouth is like one breath of air blown into a vast empty house. What little food is given is chewed very slowly. Still, it makes no difference—we feel even more hungry after eating. Even in our sleep, our dreams are haunted by food. There are those who chew noisily in their dreams. . . . Such food as mice, rats, birds, snakes, grasshoppers, must be caught and eaten secretly. It is forbidden, and if the camp guards learn about it, the prisoners will be punished."

were, or what condition you were in, you had to do the exercises.[65]

In keeping with the party dogma that society should be classless, the Communists also encouraged workers to inform on their bosses and students to inform on their teachers. The poor were encouraged to denounce the wealthy. Everywhere, those without power or authority were told to denounce the people above them. Meanwhile, anyone who had enjoyed a comfortable life in the former South Vietnam was told to confess to the crime of exploitation of their subordinates.

Some adopted this new philosophy wholeheartedly. But most simply parroted whatever doctrine they were given in hopes of gaining whatever privileges that might be available. Older city people in the south were more sophisticated than the rural, impoverished young soldiers from the north who were sent to watch over them. These urbanites were less inclined to yield to the new order, but they wisely avoided openly stonewalling the Communists, since it would likely result in a trip to a reeducation camp. Instead, they engaged in a kind of stubborn passive resistance that served their own interests by slowing the pace of the Communists' consolidation of power. In public, they appeared deferential to Communist authority, but in private they ridiculed the Communists and quietly continued operating shops and other businesses for profit, in violation of their new rulers' ideology. Frustrated at the sluggish pace of reform and anxious to subjugate the resistant south, the Communist leadership in

Hanoi decided the time had come for the formal unification of north and south.

REUNIFICATION AT LAST

After a year of nonstop effort to gain control over the south, Vietnam's leaders felt the need to formally unify the nation as a means of consolidating their power. Elections were held on April 25, 1976, for a national assembly, which was assigned the task of drawing up a new constitution. The elections were tightly controlled. There was no campaigning allowed before election day. Everyone of voting age was required to show up at the polls and select candidates from a list approved by Communist political committees. Anyone who failed to vote would lose his or her food ration card—a serious threat, since without such cards, adequate food could not be obtained.

In late June 1976, the newly elected national assembly met in Hanoi and adopted a new constitution that was virtually identical to the old constitution for North Vietnam. On July 2, the announcement was made that the country was officially unified and was to be known henceforth as the Socialist Republic of Vietnam, with Hanoi as its capital.

Despite the political unification of the nation, efforts to merge two diametrically opposed economic systems lagged. By early 1978, hard-line northern Communists had become fed up with the sluggish pace of economic reform in the south, where many privately owned businesses and shops still openly operated. To speed the pace of economic reform, the Communists seized all remaining private businesses. Tens of thousands of small business owners in Saigon found themselves impoverished by this move, since their inventory represented their only asset.

On March 31, 1978, all private enterprise was formally outlawed. Those who were left unemployed by this turn of events were to be shipped off to newly established farms, deceptively called new economic zones. These farms served a dual function. The nation's economic planners hoped that by establishing new farms, Vietnam's food supply would be increased. Also, these farms were a good place to put individuals whom the government saw as troublemakers. In all, about 4 million people were sent to the new economic zones. From overcrowded cities, people were sent to farms that had been abandoned during the war and to patches of jungle in the Central Highlands that had been cleared for farming and in the south's Mekong Delta region. Many ex-soldiers and former government officials who had just been released from reeducation camps were sent to new economic zones along with unemployed city dwellers.

Life on a new economic zone farm was difficult, especially for people who, as city dwellers, were not used to hard labor nor experienced at farming. Upon arrival, workers had to construct their own shelters and hack away layers of tough jungle growth to clear the land before any planting could begin. Many found it impossible to adjust to their new lives. More than half of the workers sent from Saigon eventually left their designated new economic zones and returned home without authorization, even though doing so meant not being able to obtain a ration card and not being given a place to live.

Downtown Saigon bustles with life in 1975. Vietnam's urban centers struggled in the new Communist economy after the war.

As a result, the five hundred new economic zone farms that were established never retained enough workers to significantly increase countrywide food production as the Communists had hoped.

VIETNAM EXODUS

Thousands of Vietnamese who might have been destined for the new economic zones never went. Instead, they chose to leave their country altogether. Approximately 130,000 Vietnamese had managed last-minute escapes via planes, helicopters, and boats when the North Vietnamese forces had closed in on Saigon, but once the Communists took over, the number of people leaving declined sharply, with only about 5,000 leaving the following year. In 1977, the number of emigrants jumped past 20,000.

This relatively small trickle of emigration became a flood in 1978 when the government began seizing small businesses and tens of thousands of merchants in the south suddenly lost both their livelihoods and their personal savings. Tens of thousands of these merchants decided to flee Vietnam to find a better future elsewhere, they hoped, in America. The sudden exodus of these merchants and their families in mid- to late 1978 caused the number of emigrants to skyrocket past 80,000.

Far from trying to prevent this exodus, Vietnam's government encouraged it. For one thing, the great majority of these merchants were ethnic Chinese, known as Viet Hoa, and the Vietnamese government considered them potentially disloyal for this reason. Moreover, Vietnam's officials were desperate to fill the nation's depleted treasury, and saw the sale of exit visas and other documents as a means of extracting any wealth that these former merchants had managed to retain following the seizure of their businesses. Small offices were even set up by the government where the Viet Hoa could purchase official exit documents with gold. The price for each adult's departure permission was set at about $1,500 in gold. This sale of departure documents proved very lucrative and brought much-needed hard currency into Vietnam's government coffers.

Once they had the necessary documents, for most of the Viet Hoa, the only means of exiting Vietnam was by sea. Viet Hoa families often spent the rest of their money securing passage on a boat. With hopes for a brighter future, they boarded vessels of all shapes and sizes. However, many among what came to be called the boat people would find that their miseries were only beginning as they began their journey to a new life.

Chapter

5 The Boat People

In response to economic reforms imposed by Vietnam's government, hundreds of thousands of anxious refugees left Vietnam by boat beginning in 1978, hoping to find new lives in America and elsewhere. Some of these emigrants managed to buy passage on commercial vessels designed for sea voyages and sailed by professionals, but the majority wound up sailing aboard badly overloaded boats that were never meant to sail more than a few miles from shore. Increasing their danger, many emigrants vastly underestimated the length of the voyage ahead and sailed away without enough food or water to sustain them for a journey that could take weeks. Out at sea, their meager provisions ran out; sometimes fuel supplies ran out as well or the engines failed, leaving the boats and their passengers at the mercy of the seas.

Some Vietnamese who owned boats were eager to cash in on the exodus by transporting emigrants to such destinations as Malaysia, Indonesia, or the Philippines. These individuals charged desperate emigrants exorbitant prices for space in their boat. Others sold them the boat outright, again for sums greater than the actual value of the vessel. Most of those wishing to leave had little, if any, knowledge of boats and were easily conned into buying vessels that were not seaworthy. Adding to the danger was the fact that these boats often were not equipped with nautical charts or compasses; in any case, the emigrants lacked the skills to use such tools properly.

Those departing set sail during all types of weather, including the monsoon season, during which they were drenched by rain and threatened by high seas and strong winds. Even in good weather, theirs would be a perilous voyage across hundreds of miles of rough open water in the South China Sea and the Gulf of Thailand. Moreover, the islands that were so often the emigrants' immediate destination were easily missed. As a result, wherever they were headed, many of the Vietnamese boat people quickly were lost at sea.

Some of the smaller boats left Vietnam so overloaded that there was no place for anyone to sit. Beset by seasickness and sun exposure, and seemingly sailing around in circles, many of the emigrants discarded traditional Vietnamese manners emphasizing civility toward one another in favor of bickering and bouts of intense anger. Parents fretted as their children began to die of dehydration; others simply became distraught over the futility of the whole situation. One refugee, Le Tran, recalled his harrowing experience aboard a twenty-foot boat loaded with sixty-three people:

> It took us twenty-one days to reach Malaysia. I will never forget that trip. . . . The second day at sea we hit a very bad storm. It was as if we were some small toy bouncing up and down. People got sick. Children cried. Then the ship's captain admitted to us that he was not as experienced a navigator as he had claimed before we left. . . . On the seventh day, our food and water were gone. People began to be very sick and argue constantly. The closeness and the weather made some crazy and we had to ignore what the crazy ones were saying.[66]

The only hope of survival for the hapless Vietnamese who found themselves stranded was rescue at sea by a passing ship. In the first months of the boat exodus, passing merchant vessels might well stop and pick up the exhausted, dehydrated refugees. Unfortunately, captains often found to their dismay that authorities at their destination were unwilling to

Vietnamese refugees escape the Communist government in a small, overloaded boat. Thousands who sought refuge outside of Vietnam suffered both at sea and in refugee camps.

DESCENT INTO CANNIBALISM

Amid the boat people exodus, a fifteen-year-old orphan named Pham jumped on a small boat leaving for Hong Kong. In his account of the fifty-two-day voyage, first told to Time *reporter Roger Ronseblatt, and reprinted in* The Vietnam Experience: The Aftermath, *Pham tells how the boat's crew and passengers resorted to cannibalism to survive.*

"The boatmaster wanted to eat me. . . . [He] told a boy who was a neighbor of mine to take a hammer and hit me on the head, so that they might eat my flesh. . . . They put a shirt over my head and they hit me with something hard. I felt the men come over to lift off the shirt. But I was still conscious. I heard the boatmaster order another man to cut my throat. At the moment they took the shirt off my head, they saw that I was conscious, and that tears were on my face. I did not know what they were thinking. Then someone said, 'Pham, do you want to live?' And I said, 'Yes, of course I want to live.' So they untied me and took me into the cabin. . . . The next day, the boy who used the hammer on me was himself found dead. After the body was discovered, the boatmaster pulled it up out of the hold. Then he cut up the body. Everyone was issued a piece of meat about two fingers wide."

allow the refugees to disembark. In such cases, the Vietnamese became the responsibility of the captain and ship's owner. As a result, the boat people increasingly found that passing freighters and other vessels would not pick them up.

INTERNATIONAL CRISIS

Still, the number of Vietnamese fleeing their homeland grew. By 1979, the boat people exodus had developed into a full-blown international crisis as more than ten thousand Vietnamese per month took to the waters to flee their country. As a humanitarian gesture, officials in Thailand, Malaysia, and other destination countries at first set up makeshift refugee camps. But as the stream of refugees continued, the camps quickly became overcrowded, taxing the limited resources of the host countries. Often, too, the citizens of the destination countries made it clear that they wanted nothing to do with the refugees. In Malaysia, for example, some residents began the practice of stoning boat people as they tried to wade ashore.

To curtail the drain on their resources and to ease tensions between their own people and the refugees, leaders from countries that had been accepting Vietnamese refugees, including Thailand, Malaysia, Singapore, Indonesia, and the Philippines, announced that they would prohibit any more boat people from landing. For people who had already been at sea for weeks, the situation became critical, since they had nowhere to go and could not survive much longer without landing.

Some Vietnamese refugees took their chances and ignored the prohibition. Sailors aboard armed patrol boats aggressively turned away these refugees as they approached the shoreline. Boatloads full of exhausted refugees frequently were towed back out to sea. There, many of the smaller boats, with their fuel gone, would be swamped by waves. In such cases, the passengers faced almost certain drowning. Sometimes, desperate refugees would maneuver their boats back toward the shoreline and then jump into the water in hopes of making it ashore despite the fact that most did not know how to swim. Refugees also resorted to deliberately sinking their boats within sight of shore patrols in hopes of being rescued.

Even if they still had fuel and provisions to last them for a time, the emigrants were often in mortal danger. Stuck out at sea with nowhere to go, the defenseless boat people became easy targets for pirates. The problem was especially serious in the Gulf of Thailand, where pirates boarded numerous boats, searched the passengers, and stole any valuables, and then raped the girls and young women. One survivor recalled, "These pirates were so young, I guess sixteen or seventeen. Each of them had a very long knife and held it to the throat of every person on the boat asking for money. They knew only a few Vietnamese words: money, dollars, gold, watch—that's it. We were so terrified."[67]

About a third of all refugee boats that left Vietnam were attacked by pirates. Girls and young women on the boats were sometimes kidnapped into a life of forced prostitution. According to Hoa Tong, a woman who witnessed one such raid,

> The pirates separated twenty women and ordered them off the boat. There were many protests. Nothing helped. People even fell overboard. It was mass confusion, hysteria and shock. They were the prettiest girls and after they were gone, all we could hear were more cries and muffled protests. They took our girls, food and water. We were left to die. Five days later a Norwegian ship picked us up. The officials said the girls that the pirates stole were taken to Ko Kra Island and sold into prostitution.[68]

In such cases there was little family members could do; the pirates often killed anyone on the boats who attempted to intervene. Even remaining passive did not guarantee one's safety. Sometimes the pirates simply robbed everyone on board and then sank the boats, leaving the passengers to drown.

Those who survived such terrible perils were often left with traumatic memories. One Vietnamese mother recalled her painful experience on the ocean in a small boat: "We couldn't move. My 2-month-old boy had a fever, and I couldn't feed him because I couldn't produce milk for him. I didn't have food to eat myself. He died. I had to put the baby in the ocean. It was the worst day of my life."[69] Such experiences were hardly unique. The United Nations estimated that up to 33 percent of all boat people perished during the ocean voyage.

A Vietnamese woman, one of many who fled by boat, shields herself and her child from the harsh sun.

REFUGEE CAMPS

In spite of the dangers at sea and the inhospitable reception they faced when they made landfall, the Vietnamese refugees kept coming. Eventually, in response to the world's outcry to the plight of the boat people, the United Nations set up refugee camps on the outlying islands of Malaysia and other remote locations where the refugees would be isolated from increasingly hostile native populations. Within months, however, condi-

tions deteriorated so badly that the camps themselves became a new humanitarian crisis. An Australian writer named Bruce Grant visited Pulau Bidong camp, located on a little island off the coast of Malaysia. He describes the scene:

> One stepped ashore into a violent, tragic, sordid, but also indestructibly resilient world. Bidong was a dangerously congested slum; a tropical island ghetto; a chunk of South Vietnamese society pre-1975, unrepentantly Capitalist, anti-Communist and predatory, grafted onto a bit of offshore Malaysia; a shantytown with a population of 42,000 confined to a living area of less than one square kilometer.[70]

Responding to this new crisis, the United Nations held an international conference in Geneva in July 1979. As an outgrowth of that meeting, the UN pressured Vietnam's government to curtail the tremendous flow of refugees. Persuading the Vietnamese government to do this was no easy task since up to this point it had been profiting handsomely from the sale of departure permissions, even though it had officially denied any involvement in such practices. Reluctantly, Vietnam agreed to cooperate with the UN and took immediate actions to stem the flow of refugees, which it had

Forgotten Children

The plight of young Amerasians, the children fathered by Americans serving in Vietnam, remained an almost forgotten outcome of the war amid the boat people exodus, as revealed in this excerpt from a 1984 article by Susanna McBee titled "The Amerasians: Tragic Legacy of Our Far East Wars" from U.S. News & World Report.

"Left behind in Asia are the mixed-race offspring of American GI's and civilians who served there and then returned home. Ethnically pure Asians often consider such children less than dirt. These youngsters are the Amerasians—the forgotten progeny of war. In South Vietnam, they are called *bui doi*—dust of life. Targets of virulent discrimination in Vietnam, Amerasians are particular scapegoats. One boy of 13, interviewed in Thailand as he awaited passage to the U.S., had dropped out of a Vietnamese school in the third grade. He had been forced to sit each day through two hours of indoctrination in which the United States was blamed for all of Vietnam's ills. 'I couldn't stand hearing how bad the U.S. is,' he complains. 'My father is American.'. . . Amerasians wanting to leave their native countries must grapple with mountains of red tape and often years of infuriating delay. Once Amerasians reach the U.S., they often have serious trouble adjusting. Half-black Amerasians do not consider themselves black but find that some Americans do. Half-white Amerasians, who do not look Asian, are frustrated when everyone they meet expects them to speak English. Mothers of Amerasians often have greater problems than their children. Some mothers think they will become rich instantly and that they will be reunited with the fathers of their youngsters. They rarely end up in the communities where the fathers live, but in a few instances, they have moved nearby. On occasion, the children show resentment when reunited with their fathers. 'It's about time,' one girl told her father. 'Why did you leave me? Why did it take so long for you to get me?'"

controlled all along. Vietnamese involved in arranging escapes were now jailed. Amid the sudden clampdown and resulting climate of fear, the number of boat people drastically declined, dropping to an average of fifty thousand in 1980–1981 and falling even more sharply over the next few years.

Meanwhile, upwards of 400,000 worn-out Vietnamese were now stuck inside squalid refugee camps throughout Southeast Asia awaiting resettlement. The UN addressed this issue by asking several Western nations to accept a large number of Vietnamese immigrants to ease the overcrowding. The United States agreed to increase its monthly quota of Southeast Asian immigrants to 14,000. However, the refugees faced long delays in negotiating a maze of bureaucratic red tape before they could leave. For example, each refugee first had to obtain proper documentation allowing him or her to settle in a specific country, such as the United States, France, Canada, or Australia.

Thousands of refugees sat by in frustrating idleness for months, sometimes years, waiting for their chance to leave the camps. On many occasions, when they finally received permission to leave, it was not to the country that was their first choice. When this happened to someone whose relatives had left Vietnam earlier and were already established in their new homes, the unfortunate refugee had to face the possibility of being separated from relatives for a long time.

Most of the refugees wanted to go to America. They either already had family members living there or had heard that opportunities to make a new life abounded in America.

Life in America

Those Vietnamese refugees who did end up in America found the freedom and opportunity they had yearned for, but they also found themselves in a fast-paced, impersonal society, light years removed from the homespun family culture they had known. For some, life in America was so completely different from the life they had known that, in the words of one immigrant, arriving in the United States seemed like "stepping onto the moon."[71] Although they were thrilled to be living in America at last, many Vietnamese immigrants also felt an intense sadness at having left their homeland behind so abruptly. Most of the refugees still had family members in Vietnam and believed there was little chance they would ever see them again. Duong Quang Son, who left Vietnam at age sixteen, revealed how he felt about being separated from his family upon his arrival in America: "Every night I cry for Vietnam. I remember and I cry. In the darkness my memories turn to tears. There are tears for my dad and my mom and for my brother and my sisters, and for all those who could not run away."[72]

The immigrants' experiences differed in large measure according to their circumstances prior to leaving Vietnam. The first wave of Vietnamese immigrants to America, totaling about 130,000 people, had left Vietnam in 1975, as the Communists were closing in on Saigon. This group included many of South Vietnam's elite, such as high-ranking government and military officers, and well-educated professionals, including lawyers, doctors, and professors. Many of them spoke English. Moreover, many had befriended Americans in Vietnam, and these friends helped them upon their arrival in the United States by providing moral support and by assisting them in finding jobs and places to live.

A much smaller group of Vietnamese, numbering about 43,000, arrived in America between 1975 and 1977. These refugees tended to have less education than the first wave of immigrants and were more likely to have been peasant

A South Vietnamese and an American soldier share a friendly embrace. American soldiers tried to help South Vietnamese friends who immigrated to the United States.

farmers or fishermen. These newer arrivals also lacked the advantage of well-connected American friends, and so were largely on their own as they sought to settle in their new home.

The boat people who began leaving Vietnam in 1978, numbering well over 300,000, faced the greatest challenge of all. A significant number of this third wave were poorly educated, lacked marketable skills, and spoke no English. Adding to the difficulties for this third wave of immigrants was the fact that America in the late 1970s was in the midst of a serious economic recession. Jobs were already scarce, so most Americans were not anxious to welcome a big influx of potential competitors for those jobs.

For Vietnamese families, the daily pressures of trying to cope with their new lives in America put extra stress on traditional parent-child relationships, as this *USA Today* magazine report noted:

> If [Vietnamese] parents are expressing difficulty in coping with the contrasts between the relative openness of the new society and their traditional parental roles, children face a set of conflicting expectations and often confusing choices. In addition to such practical issues of adjustment as learning a new language, becoming

DIMINISHED PRIDE

For Vietnamese men, coming from a centuries-old patriarchal society, adjusting to their lowered status as poorly paid immigrants in America proved difficult. This excerpt from a 1993 USA Today *magazine article titled "The Unsettling Resettlement of Vietnamese Boat People," by Michael P. Smith and Bernadette Tarallo, identifies some of these difficulties.*

One community development specialist the authors interviewed notes, "There's a lot of real frustrations for [Vietnamese] men [in America]. They are no longer able to assume that dominant role, because they are not breadwinners anymore; they aren't held in respect anymore because they don't know English, and they can't get along, and that is a big problem, not only between women and men, but between parents and the children. [Their children say,] 'Oh mom and dad, you're so old fashioned. What do you know? You don't even speak English; why do I have to listen to you?'. . . It's something that Americans would say their teenagers have been saying for years, but these people are not used to it. . . . They are used to the old subordination to the parents, and that is the norm, and that's what's expected, and that's how they've been trained. So then it just throws them for a loop when the kids are out of control now."

Vietnamese men, especially older men, had difficulty adjusting to the American way of life.

accustomed to the U.S. school system, and meeting new peers, they face a host of social-psychological issues in straddling or negotiating conflicting Vietnamese values and expectations of filial respect and authority. They also must confront the expectations of independence, self-satisfaction, and questioning of authority to a point encouraged by their new society.[73]

Most young Vietnamese chose to study hard and earn extra money to help their struggling parents. Others, however, succumbed to the temptation to engage in criminal activities. In Southern California, gang violence reared its ugly head as youths from rival Vietnamese gangs began attacking each other on the streets. Gang members also began targeting innocent Vietnamese, breaking into their homes, beating them, and robbing them of whatever money and jewelry they might have.

Gradually, the Vietnamese in America formed small communities within American cities. Places like Little Saigon in Westminster, California, featured shops, restaurants, and other businesses that catered to an almost exclusively Vietnamese clientele. Still, many Vietnamese in America experienced a profound sense of grief over what they had lost and despair regarding their current situation. One news report noted the experience of Vietnamese living in Westminster's Little Saigon:

Many of the older immigrants were soldiers on a losing side or were jailed after the North's victory, or both. And these veterans, like their American counterparts, suffer from post-traumatic

stress disorders and severe bouts of depression. They have also seen little upward mobility in their new land: Unlike other East Asian groups in America, the Vietnamese are primarily working class, struggling to survive in poor urban ghettos. "There's a lot of personal baggage among people coming from a country at war," says Xuyen Matsuda, a clinical social worker who deals with Vietnamese-American families. "I'm concerned about the chronic feeling of powerlessness people have felt since coming from Vietnam," she says. Some 40 percent of her caseload speaks only Vietnamese, mostly low-income parents and single mothers with young kids. She treats them for depression, domestic abuse, and post-traumatic stress disorders.[74]

Within the Vietnamese community, a generational divide gradually emerged between those who had fled war-torn Vietnam and their offspring and those who were subsequently born in the United States, as one newsmagazine noted:

Older people still regard America as a refuge [while] younger people regard it as a new home. Asked "would you go back and live in Vietnam if the government changed?" Nam Tran [who fled Vietnam] says she would, but her children [raised in America] would not. Although Vietnamese children often finish first in Californian high schools, their parents and grandparents sometimes live miserable lives. . . . The humiliation for some is that they cannot talk to their English-speaking grandchildren.[75]

Although their offspring typically expressed little interest in their ancestral homeland, many older refugees, who retained a faint hope of someday returning to Vietnam, maintained a keen interest in events there. They would read Vietnamese-language newspapers and gather with fellow Vietnamese refugees to discuss postwar Vietnamese politics. As it turned out, they had much to talk about, as peace in newly unified Vietnam proved short-lived. By the late 1970s, Vietnamese troops were on the march again, and once again, the country would have to face foreign troops on its soil.

Chapter

6 Vietnam Takes Cambodia

The year 1975, which had seen the fall of South Vietnam, also saw neighboring Cambodia plunge into turmoil with the rise of a mysterious leader named Pol Pot. He was the head of an armed revolutionary movement known as the Khmer Rouge, meaning Red (Communist) Cambodians. The Khmer Rouge included thousands of teenage peasant warriors who were fiercely loyal to Pol Pot. On April 17, 1975, after five years of fighting, Pol Pot's young warriors had marched victoriously into Cambodia's capital of Phnom Penh and effectively seized control of the entire country.

Pol Pot, like many Cambodians, harbored a deep ethnic hatred of the Vietnamese. The Vietnamese likewise had long harbored an intense dislike of their Cambodian neighbors. Historically, Vietnam had invaded Cambodia from time to time, and the fact that the Vietnamese now had a huge and well-equipped army only heightened the Cambodians' fear and mistrust. Therefore, upon seizing power in Cambodia, one of Pol Pot's first actions was to expel all ethnic Vietnamese living in his country—a total of some 200,000 individuals. Eventually, Pol Pot would take even more drastic action against Vietnam, but first he intended to consolidate his power and fulfill his life-long mission to remake Cambodia into a utopian peasant society—communism in its purest form.

To begin the process, Pol Pot proclaimed Cambodia to be in Year Zero, meaning that all knowledge of the past was to be blotted out and time started over inside Cambodia, which he renamed the Democratic Republic of Kampuchea. To create this new utopia, every facet of Cambodian society was to be purified. To this end, capitalism, all elements of city life, religion, Western culture, and any other foreign influences were to be extinguished. By means that Pol Pot never really articulated, this process would allow him to create a truly classless society in Cambodia.

MADNESS OF THE KILLING FIELDS

The dismantling of Cambodian society began immediately. Cambodia was swiftly cut off from the outside world. Within hours of taking over, the Khmer Rouge had expelled all foreigners and abruptly shut down all embassies. The speaking of foreign languages was banned. Newspapers and television stations were shuttered. Radios and bicycles were confiscated. Mail and telephone services were eliminated. Money and all private property were outlawed. All businesses and schools were closed, practice of all religions prohibited, and health care eliminated.

Incredible scenes of forced evacuations occurred throughout the country as Cambodians living in cities and towns were driven from their homes and into the countryside to begin new lives as peasants in Pol Pot's model society. In Phnom Penh, Pol Pot's ruthless young warriors, some as young as twelve years old, strutted about the streets brazenly waving automatic rifles and other weapons as they forced 2 million city dwellers to leave the capital. One Cambodian, Someth May, described the chaotic exodus he had witnessed in which up to twenty thousand people died:

> We moved very slowly in the heat of the day. Some people were carrying their possessions on their backs or on bicycles. Others had handcarts which they pushed and pulled. There were overloaded *cyclas* [bicycle pedicabs] with families balancing on them and parents pushing. . . . Children cried out that they were being squashed in the crowd. Everywhere people were losing their relatives.[76]

Upon arriving in the countryside, exhausted survivors of all ages were put into forced labor on large parcels of land.

Pol Pot led the Communist Khmer Rouge to victory in Cambodia in 1975, subjecting Cambodians to unimaginable horrors.

Workdays lasted fourteen to eighteen hours, with people being given only a bowl or two of watery rice porridge to eat. Former city dwellers, totally unaccustomed to farm life, began dying by the thousands each day from overwork and malnutrition. Humans performed brute labor in the fields that was normally done by farm animals. One survivor of this time recalled, "We didn't have any oxen so we formed a team of eight men to pull the plough. Several of my comrades, exhausted by this work, began spitting up blood and died."[77]

Death also came in the form of murderous purges conducted by the Khmer Rouge in an attempt to exterminate all remnants of Cambodia's old society. Professionals such as teachers, lawyers, and doctors were the first to be targeted.

EXECUTION LESSON

All rules, regulations, and punishments in Cambodia were issued by Khmer Rouge soldiers in the name of Angka, Pol Pot's shadowy political organization. Children in remote villages were told to love and obey Angka, not their parents, and were even forced to watch executions of those who supposedly disobeyed Angka. Roeun Sam, a young girl at the time, remembered one such execution in Children of Cambodia's Killing Fields *(by Dith Pran).*

"All the kids like me were forced by the leader to sit in front to see one of the prisoners. Angka [i.e., the Khmer Rouge soldier] said, 'If anyone cries or shows empathy or compassion for this person, they will be punished by receiving the same treatment.' Angka told someone to get the prisoner on his knees. The prisoner had to confess what he had done wrong. Then the prisoner began to talk but he didn't confess anything. Instead, he screamed. 'God, I did not do anything wrong. Why are they doing this to me? I work day and night, never complain, and even though I get sick and I have a hard time getting around, I satisfy you so you won't kill people. I never thought to betray Angka. This is injustice. I have done nothing wrong!' Suddenly one of them hit him from the back, pushed him, and he fell face to the ground. It was raining. We sat in the rain, and then the rain became blood. He was hit with a shovel and then he went unconscious and began to have a seizure. Then Angka took out a sharp knife and cut the man from his breastbone all the way down to his stomach. They took out his organs. When I saw this I felt so shocked, like I was blind. It felt like they were hitting me just as they hit the prisoner. The person that cut him open took a sharp piece of wire and stuck it in what I think was the liver and bowels. They tied the organs with wire on the handlebars of a bicycle and biked away, leaving a bloody trail. Angka calmly told us over the microphone, 'All girls and boys, you have seen with your own eyes. If someone feels compassion or sympathy for the enemy that has just died, then you will be punished just like him.'"

Simply wearing a pair of eyeglasses was enough to get one killed, since doing so was considered by the Khmer Rouge to be a sign of elitism. Former soldiers and government officials were next. Not only did the Khmer Rouge kill these officials, but they murdered innocent family members as well. One youth, who was fourteen when Pol Pot came to power, watched the Khmer Rouge kill members of his family:

> Three months after my grandfather [an ex-soldier] was murdered, the [Khmer Rouge] soldiers took my brother and brother-in-law. They were tied up and taken two or three miles into the jungle. This time I followed, sneaking through the undergrowth so that no one would see me. I watched as my brothers were forced to dig a large hole while the soldiers held guns to their heads. I remember one soldier saying to the other, "We will save our bullets." Then they took big bamboo shoots and beat my brothers again and again until they were dead. Their bodies were kicked into the hole. Their grave was not far from where my grandfather was killed.[78]

The Khmer Rouge demanded total submission and killed anyone suspected of even a trace of disloyalty to Pol Pot or anyone accused of what they called the "crime of individualism." To survive, one had to behave like a humble, obedient peasant, and follow all Khmer Rouge orders no matter how bizarre they seemed.

Throughout the countryside, unsupervised gatherings of more than two people were forbidden. All children were taken from their parents and placed in communes, where they were closely supervised by the Khmer Rouge. In these communes, the youngsters were subjected to brainwashing designed to make them believe that Pol Pot and the Khmer Rouge were their new family. As a result, many young Cambodians developed a slavish devotion to the new regime. According to one eyewitness,

> One group of more than twenty youths aged about fifteen was arrested. They did not try to run away. They just said: "I am faithful to the [Khmer Rouge] Party. I obey the Party. If I die, I die faithful to the Party and loving it." And all those youngsters were executed. The Party was a god to them.[79]

TURNING TO VIETNAM

Once he had achieved absolute power inside Cambodia, Pol Pot turned his attention eastward, toward the nearly four-hundred-mile-long border with Vietnam where tensions had long been simmering. Pol Pot, reportedly delusional by now, convinced himself that an attack by Vietnam was imminent. To protect Cambodia and to harass any Vietnamese, Pol Pot stationed his Khmer Rouge troops along the border. As Pol Pot's forces arrived, border tensions quickly escalated, and sporadic shooting between Vietnamese soldiers and the Khmer Rouge broke out.

In early 1977, Pol Pot decided to stage a preemptive military strike and sent four divisions of Khmer Rouge troops across

KILLER BOYS

Many of the murderous Khmer Rouge soldiers were actually young boys who were eager to please their new masters and would do anything to gain approval, as Someth May recounted in his autobiography, Cambodian Witness.

"One day as we were harvesting the rice, we heard screams. A member of the resistance had been caught. He was brought back on a pole, like a pig to the slaughterhouse. Behind him came his [fourteen-year-old] son, Comrade Thol. He had a thorny stick in his hand, with which he was whipping his father as they went. The father squealed in agony. His uniform was drenched with blood. They made their way towards the headquarters. News soon spread that Comrade Thol had killed his whole family—his father first. His mother watched while he slit his throat. Then Comrade Thol killed his six-month-old sister. Finally he killed his mother. He was rewarded with an AK-47 [rifle], of which he was very proud. He came round the fields to show it off."

Young boys wield powerful M16 rifles in their role as Khmer Rouge soldiers.

the border. During the attack, the Khmer Rouge slaughtered entire families of Vietnamese civilians without provocation. Responding to what it labeled Pol Pot's aggression, Vietnam massed its own troops and prepared to retaliate.

VIETNAM INVADES

In December 1977 eight divisions of Vietnamese infantry, supported by tanks and artillery, roared into Cambodia, expecting a swift victory. At first, the Vietnamese easily pushed back Pol Pot's troops. But after falling back, Pol Pot's forces managed to regroup and then put up surprisingly stiff resistance to the better-equipped Vietnamese. As the momentum slowly shifted in their favor, the Cambodians skillfully used the age-old tactic of hit-and-run guerrilla raids to wear down the Vietnamese invaders. This was the same tactic the Vietnamese themselves had once used so effectively against American troops in Vietnam.

Now, the Vietnamese army found itself in a predicament similar to the one the Americans had faced in Vietnam. Vietnam's army was no longer the nimble force of jungle warriors who were fanatically loyal to their leader. Instead, the army had grown into a gigantic, mechanized force that relied on conventional military tactics to fight an unconventional jungle war.

The large armored columns of Vietnamese personnel carriers, tanks, and infantry slowed and then became bogged down in the jungle, providing inviting targets for swift-footed Khmer Rouge fighters who would quickly strike and then vanish. One military analyst re-

marked at the time, "The Viets are making U.S. mistakes. They were much better when their only equipment was an AK47 [rifle] and a pair of thousand-milers [rubber sandals]."[80]

In addition, many of the same dynamics that had so hampered the American forces now hindered the Vietnamese. For example, morale problems reduced the effectiveness of the Vietnamese army. Amid an increasing death toll, Vietnamese troops became tentative, reluctant fighters unwilling to risk casualties. Making matters worse, to avoid provoking neighboring China, which was closely allied with Cambodia, the Vietnamese leadership was holding back its army's full might.

Seizing the initiative, Pol Pot's Khmer Rouge fighters forced the Vietnamese into a slow withdrawal from Cambodia. The Cambodians' celebrations over this apparent victory were premature, however, because the Vietnamese withdrawal was only temporary. Vietnam's top military leaders were not about to let the Cambodians' victory stand. They set out to crush the Cambodians by launching a second, much bigger invasion. And this time, they did not hold back—a decision that would have significant consequences for Vietnam.

Vietnam's second invasion commenced on December 25, 1978, with 200,000 Vietnamese soldiers assaulting Cambodian positions on four big fronts. The Vietnamese tactics closely resembled the lightning quick attacks that had been so effective against South Vietnamese forces back in 1975. But now, the Vietnamese were stronger, their weaponry even including Russian-built fighter jets and captured American armaments, such

as airplanes and heli-
copters. In the face of
this onslaught, Pol Pot's
troops, poorly equipped
by comparison, began to
fall back. As they had
done in 1975, Vietnam's
commanders quickly took
advantage of their ene-
my's disarray and rushed
to capture all of their
primary objectives, then
dashed toward the main
prize, Cambodia's capi-
tal of Phnom Penh.

Interestingly, the Viet-
namese were aided in
part by Cambodia's civil-
ian populace. For many
Cambodians, who had
long suffered under Pol
Pot's brutal regime, the
invading Vietnamese sol-
diers were liberators.
Len Kath, a survivor,
remembered,

Young Khmer Rouge soldiers were instrumental in carrying out Pol Pot's campaign of terror.

> Who would ever think
> we would welcome
> the Vietnamese army
> to Cambodia? For
> many centuries we
> fought each other, then we watched as
> they entered the country and we were
> glad and happy to see them. They
> took away the Pol Pot butchers. When
> the Vietnamese conquered, we hoped
> for the best, for anything that would
> be different, that would be better.[81]

Pol Pot's troops scattered as the Vietnamese approached the city of Phnom
Penh. On January 7, 1979, the Vietnamese

easily overran the deserted city. Pol Pot
himself escaped into the rugged mountains of western Cambodia with a large
number of loyal Khmer Rouge troops.
From remote jungle camps, these guerrillas
would continue to harass their foes, but
they would not return to lead their nation.

INVADERS SEEN AS LIBERATORS

The invasion of Cambodia by Vietnamese troops was universally condemned. At the time, however, Cambodians who had endured years of terror under the Pol Pot regime felt differently, as survivor Teeda Butt Mam states in her book (with Joan D. Criddle) To Destroy You Is No Loss: The Odyssey of a Cambodian Family.

"Everywhere the Vietnamese went they were hailed as liberators. Their lightning invasion was totally unexpected by the populace, yet so welcome. The outside world, however, still not believing how horrendous conditions had been, was vehement in its censure of the 'invaders.' The Vietnamese correctly called Cambodia 'hell on earth,' and stated that they planned to free us from the oppression under which we labored. My family did not credit Vietnam with such humanitarian motives, but we, and the rest of our countrymen, were deeply grateful that the secondary effect of Vietnam's drive for expansion had been liberation from our bondage. . . . Most people did not stop to ask what life would be like under the new leaders. They enjoyed the moment. The Khmer Rouge were routed; they could obtain food. They were free to find long-missing loved ones. Hopes soared. Life under Pol Pot had been so repressive that people willingly switched allegiance to the invaders."

This victory came at a huge price for the Vietnamese. Nations from Western Europe and Southeast Asia, including Japan, condemned what they considered brazen aggression and cut off hundreds of millions of dollars in badly needed economic aid to Vietnam. More ominously, China, which had also been supporting Vietnam economically, stopped its aid and chastised its neighbor to the south, vowing to teach Vietnam a lesson.

CHINA INVADES VIETNAM

That lesson was not long in coming. On February 17, 1979, eight divisions of China's People's Liberation Army crossed the border into northern Vietnam. At first, the terrain favored the Vietnamese. Chinese troops struggled up steep hillsides and through treacherous mountain passes. As they did so, they were under constant attack from Vietnamese defenders who held positions overlooking the roads the Chinese were using. Still, some eighty-five thousand Chinese soldiers, traveling on foot and in tanks, had advanced nearly sixteen kilometers into Vietnam by the end of the second day.

After this initial success, the Chinese paused for three days to get resupplied and then continued their southward march deeper into Vietnam. At Lang Son, a city located 130 kilometers north of Hanoi, a crucial battle erupted. Vietnamese troops positioned themselves on several hills surrounding the city and once again had the advantage of being on the high ground. But the Chinese relentlessly shelled the Vietnamese positions and then overran them using tanks and infantry, and Lang Son fell on March 2. The Chinese took surrounding areas a few days later. Now, the road to Hanoi, the capital of Vietnam, lay wide open.

At this point, however, China's leaders called off their attack, passing up the opportunity to advance on Hanoi and possibly conquer Vietnam altogether. Instead, they announced that their troops were withdrawing from Vietnam. China's leaders claimed that they had achieved their objectives, but experts contend that Chinese concern about the world reaction to their aggression played a major role in their withdrawal. In any case, the People's Liberation Army slowly headed northward, back toward China.

But the retreating Chinese did not go home quietly. As they departed, they destroyed bridges and railroads. They also wrecked a big phosphorus mine that supplied raw materials for the

Vietnamese families flee Dung Ho in an attempt to escape encroaching Chinese troops in February 1979.

manufacture of fertilizer. In addition, Chinese soldiers stole just about anything of value from Vietnamese civilians they encountered. Vietnam's leaders issued statements protesting this crude behavior but took no action that might impede the Chinese withdrawal. By March 15, China's withdrawal from Vietnam was complete.

DIFFICULT OCCUPATION

China's invasion of Vietnam cost an estimated sixty thousand Vietnamese lives, two-thirds of them civilian, and another fifteen thousand Chinese lives, yet the incursion failed utterly in its stated objective of teaching Vietnam to stay within its borders. For the next ten years, the Vietnamese attempted to maintain their occupation of Cambodia and pacify its population. To administer the country, they installed a pro-Vietnamese government consisting of Khmer Rouge defectors. Some 160,000 Vietnamese soldiers were then permanently stationed inside Cambodia, providing security for the puppet government and fending off sporadic attacks by remnants of the Khmer Rouge.

Vietnam found that administering Cambodia as a client state was made difficult by old national grudges. Many Cambodians had initially been grateful to the Vietnamese for ousting Pol Pot. Over time, however, the long-standing ethnic hatred between Cambodians and Vietnamese gradually resurfaced and the Cambodians wanted the Vietnamese to go home. When it became apparent that the Vietnamese had no intention of leaving, an armed movement sprang to life with the

goal of driving out the Vietnamese. Members of three groups joined together to form a new resistance movement, including remnants of Pol Pot's Khmer Rouge, members of a non-Communist group known as the Khmer People's National Liberation, and another group that was still loyal to Cambodia's pre-1975 monarchy. In all, there were about fifty thousand guerrilla fighters in this group, which called itself the Coalition Government of Democratic Kampuchea. To arm itself, the coalition welcomed shipments of weapons from China and other Asian nations that were opposed to what amounted to Vietnam's continued occupation of Cambodia.

By the early 1980s, the Vietnamese found themselves mired in Cambodia, just as the French, and then the Americans, had been stuck in Vietnam. Just as the Vietnamese themselves had done in dealing with foreigners, the guerrillas in Cambodia avoided large-scale confrontations with the heavily armed Vietnamese. Instead, they resorted to hit-and-run raids and also planted numerous mines, which took a heavy toll among Vietnamese foot soldiers. These tactics greatly limited Vietnam's war-making options. One Vietnamese officer in Cambodia commented at the time, "If we send out a five- or six-man team, it runs the risk of ambush. If we send a battalion, they'll make so much noise that they'll never find the enemy. So most of the time we use a company [about one hundred men]."[82]

An on-the-scene news report in 1983 assessed the effectiveness of Vietnamese troops in Cambodia:

Here at this jungle base just inside Kampuchea one gets a close-up view of how anti-Vietnamese rebels are bleeding Hanoi's occupation army in a relentless campaign of hit-and-run warfare. From camps such as Ampil, nestled along the poorly marked border with Thailand, guerrillas launch strikes against Vietnamese forces all across the western part of Kampuchea. . . . When confronted by superior power, many guerrillas sometimes choose to flee to safety in Thailand, much as the Viet Cong used sanctuaries in Laos and [Cambodia] more than a decade ago. . . . The Vietnamese Army trying to subdue this [guerrilla] revolt hardly compares with the military machine that crushed South Vietnam in 1975 and overran [Cambodia] in 1978. The crack veterans of those days have been replaced by [draftees] from the defeated South. Morale is low and the desertion rate high.[83]

Vietnamese troops would attack the guerrillas' strongholds each year during the dry season that lasted from December to May. But coalition guerrillas simply fell back and escaped into neighboring Thailand. From their Thai jungle camps, the guerrillas regrouped

Small jungle enclosures like this, here being inspected by Vietnamese soldiers, became military strongholds for anti-Vietnamese forces in the early 1980s.

and harassed any Vietnamese troops that pursued them. When the wet season arrived, the guerrillas then sneaked back into Cambodia and resumed their deadly hit-and-run raids against the Vietnamese.

RELUCTANT WITHDRAWAL

Year after year, the enormous expense of keeping more than 100,000 occupying troops inside Cambodia drained Vietnam's already inadequate financial resources. Up to a third of Vietnam's annual budget was going to defense spending, supporting an army totaling some 1.2 million soldiers. Adding to Vietnam's economic woes, the nations that had previously cut off economic aid when Vietnam first invaded Cambodia refused to restore that help as long as Vietnamese troops remained inside the country. With little in the way of hard currency, Vietnam's annual inflation rate skyrocketed past 400 percent, making everyday household necessities prohibitively expensive for most Vietnamese. Life in Vietnam had become backward and miserable, as this 1985 article in *U.S. News & World Report* noted:

> Vietnam is beset by hopeless poverty and bogged down in a costly war in neighboring [Cambodia] that leaves the homeland even worse off economically than during the 16 years in which it battled the United States. . . . Repairs to Vietnam's war-damaged infrastructure go begging. Many roads have been reduced to rutted tracks unrepaired since U.S. bombing.

Travel is measured in days instead of hours. The 1,000-mile railroad trip between Ho Chi Minh City and Hanoi takes three days and three nights, with trains in the north that are pulled by antiquated steam locomotives—each of them carrying a red star as a symbol of Communist authority. Widespread inefficiency complicates recovery. Labor-saving machinery, widely available elsewhere, is hard to find. Instead, armies of peasants in conical hats brave monsoon rains to dig out silted irrigation ditches by hand, while cadres [local Communist Party members] urge them to work.[84]

The only country still interested in helping Vietnam after it conquered Cambodia was the Soviet Union. In 1978, Vietnam and the Soviet Union had signed a twenty-five year economic and military friendship pact that resulted in nearly $1 billion worth of aid flowing into Vietnam. For its part of the bargain, Vietnam allowed Soviet warships and submarines unhindered access to its deepwater ports, thus giving the Soviets an important naval outpost in Southeast Asia.

By the late 1980s, however, the Soviet Union itself was beginning to experience serious financial problems as its unwieldy planned economy teetered under the burden of inefficient factories turning out expensive armaments or shoddy consumer goods that nobody would buy. With little cash to spare, the Soviets finally quit sending aid to Vietnam altogether. With their last economic lifeline severed, people in Vietnam began to suffer even more, as this 1988 magazine report noted:

In the lowlands of central Vietnam, midway between the two deltas, hunger is more than a vague fear—it is a daily reality. . . . A few miles south of Hue, Vo Van Giap, a one-time South Vietnamese Army soldier, pauses at the edge of a rice paddy harvested by a small collective. His five children "do not get enough to eat," he says, and he has to trek miles into the hills rising to the west in search of firewood to sell on the market in order to make a bare living. . . . With about 4 million people now facing starvation, Vietnamese officials acknowledge the need for "emergency" shipments of food and fertilizer.[85]

Soviet and Vietnamese leaders celebrate the tenth anniversary of Vietnam's Communist victory. Within a decade, the Soviet Union had stopped providing Vietnam with financial help.

Out of dire necessity, Vietnam's leaders realized they needed to end their country's decade-long isolation and make new friends in the world. But before they could establish those new links with countries in the West and perhaps even with China, Vietnam first needed to withdraw its troops from Cambodia. Thus, in May 1988, Vietnam's leaders announced that fifty thousand Vietnamese soldiers would soon be coming home. Two months later, the first peace talks occurred in Cambodia between members of the anti-Vietnamese guerrilla coalition and the Vietnamese-allied government. By September 1989, all of Vietnam's troops had exited Cambodia. After the withdrawal, various political factions in Cambodia held talks and agreed to be led by a supreme national council. To assure a measure of stability, the United Nations sent in peacekeepers and also supervised elections to prevent a return to power by Pol Pot's Khmer Rouge.

The withdrawal from Cambodia after ten years of occupation provided immediate benefits for Vietnam. It eliminated the financial drain associated with keeping so many troops inside Cambodia. Perhaps even more significantly, as Vietnam proved itself committed to peace, countries in Western Europe and Southeast Asia began providing much-needed economic aid and started investing in the country. But in opening itself to the West after so many years spent as a closed society, Vietnam clearly was about to enter a new and possibly frightening era.

Chapter

7 New Problems, Old Solutions

The arrival into Vietnam's tightly controlled society of freewheeling profit-minded businesspeople from wealthy countries in Western Europe and Southeast Asia was a mixed blessing for the nation's Communist leaders. On the one hand, the outsiders could inject desperately needed money into Vietnam's cash-starved economy. However, the danger remained that a significant capitalist presence would undo years of efforts to remake the nation according to socialist ideals. Worse, Western ideas of democracy and individualism threatened the leaders' very grasp on power.

The year 2000 marked the twenty-fifth anniversary of Communist rule in Vietnam. But in the quarter-century since the nation's unification, the Socialist Republic of Vietnam had remained one of the poorest countries on earth, burdened by a host of seemingly intractable economic, political, and social problems. The country's population had doubled since the war ended in 1975, straining Vietnam's economic resources past their limits. Other economic problems included outmoded and inefficient factories, low worker productivity, and high inflation. Chronic food shortages meant that some people went hungry; meanwhile, government officials allowed the privileged few

to get rich. Added to these problems was the stubborn reluctance of people in the south to fully embrace communism, meaning that, in reality, the nation was still only partially unified.

Beset by so many problems, the Socialist Republic of Vietnam had thus stagnated from its first days onward. Vietnam's prime minister, Pham Van Dong, had frankly admitted to historian Stanley Karnow in 1981, "Yes, we defeated the United States. But now we are plagued by problems. We do not have enough to eat. We are a poor, underdeveloped nation. [You know,] waging a war is simple, but running a country is very difficult."[86]

ECONOMIC REFORM

As early as 1986, Vietnam's leaders had realized that their economy was not growing enough to keep pace with the nation's expanding population. That year, Communist delegates to the Sixth Party Congress approved a sweeping reform package known as *Doi Moi* in Vietnamese, meaning "renovation." The reforms included permitting a limited return to free enterprise. Farmers and local craftspeople could now sell their goods at

Though the year 2000 signified the twenty-fifth anniversary of Communist rule in Vietnam, the country has turned to capitalism to boost its economy.

the marketplace and keep the proceeds of those sales. The production of Vietnamese goods for export was also encouraged to bring in badly needed foreign cash. An American news report at the time took note of how this remarkable turn of events represented an acknowledgment of defeat on the part of Vietnam's Communist leaders:

> Thirteen years after a North Vietnamese tank rolled through the gates of Saigon's Independence Palace, Vietnam's Communist rulers are openly waving the economic equivalent of a white flag. At the pivotal Sixth Party Congress . . . a new leadership wrested control of the politburo from contemporaries of Ho Chi Minh. In a historic reversal of dogma, Party General Secretary Nguyen Van Linh, 74, has begun acknowledging that a strong dose of capitalism is essential to revive Vietnam's moribund economy.[87]

The economic reforms of 1986 were accompanied by political reforms that allowed more decision making at the local level, rather than by party functionaries in Hanoi. In addition, Vietnam's leaders freed over six thousand political prisoners, including individuals who had served in South Vietnam's government and military and had been held captive ever since 1975 for refusing to reconcile. Restrictions on Vietnam's state-censored press were also eased somewhat as part of the reforms.

Some hard-line Communists in the government who were opposed to any sort of liberalization went out of their way to deliberately slow the pace of reform. Lower-level bureaucrats delayed local implementation of reforms by taking as much time as possible in reviewing required paperwork and granting administrative approvals. As a result of such determined obstruction, Vietnam in the late 1980s was still a nation in which 80 percent of the population lived in the countryside and the per capita income was less than $200 a year. People were once again leaving the country by the thousands; in 1989, for example, seventy-five thousand people left Vietnam in search of new lives in America and elsewhere. Unlike the boat people exodus a decade earlier, most of them had exit visas in hand and were going to join relatives already living abroad. Some, however, who could not legally exit the country left by sea, spurring a mini–boat people exodus, with a few thousand leaving each month. Their departure was just another indicator that Viet-

nam's economic outlook was bleak. By this time, Vietnam's leaders realized that their country was spiraling toward financial ruin. They decided to take bold new steps to save their economy from collapse.

According to the economic reforms of 1986, locals like this boat vendor, are now able to sell their goods and keep the profits.

Reaching Out to America

By 1991, with economic aid from the former Soviet Union at an end, Vietnam's leaders decided the time had come to reestablish their nation's ties to their former archenemy, the United States. For the first time, the Vietnamese offered to fully cooperate in the search for remains of U.S. soldiers missing in action. They also agreed to consider releasing any remaining detainees from reeducation camps.

THE SEARCH FOR VIETNAM'S MIAs

Though Americans have been searching for remains of soldiers missing in Vietnam for decades, the Vietnamese are just beginning to look for theirs, as shown in this excerpt from a 1995 news article by Kristin Huckshorn titled "Vietnamese Hunt Their Own MIAs—150,000 of Them."

"'I want to see my son,' said Nguyen Thi Cam, 84, mother of a Viet Cong guerrilla killed in 1968. 'I have been told that he died. But I want to see for myself so that I can be sure it is my son. Otherwise, deep down in my heart, I have a little hope that he is alive.' When President Clinton announced on [July 11] that he had restored diplomatic relations with Vietnam, he cited as the paramount reason its help in accounting for 1,618 Americans still listed as missing from the war in that country. Now, Vietnamese families are renewing personal efforts and pushing their government to accelerate searches for the remains of more than 150,000 of their own soldiers who did not return home. . . . That renewed effort is producing results. Two mass graves of Viet Cong soldiers have been discovered in Ho Chi Minh City. One, near a runway at the city's airport, contained remains of 116 bodies, the largest such grave found in recent years. Said Tran Van Ban, 51, a former Viet Cong doctor who now lives in Ho Chi Minh City and has become the government's leading hunter: 'We have noticed that the Americans come halfway around the world to find the remains of their fallen comrades. . . . It makes us think about our own comrades. Have we done enough?' . . . As modernization improves the lives of ordinary Vietnamese, it is changing the country's landscape. . . . 'Old marks are being buried,' said Ban. 'The areas we know about are disappearing with time and development. If we come much later, the bones will have turned to dust.'"

These moves coincided with increasing calls on the part of American businesspeople to end the trade embargoes against Vietnam that had been in place since the war's end in 1975. Companies from Western Europe and Japan were already exploring investment opportunities inside Vietnam, including the building of factories and other facilities, drawn by the country's plentiful cheap labor and abundant natural resources. American business leaders also wanted to get in on what they saw as a bonanza of pent-up consumer demand. As a result, a number of influential American corporate leaders asked newly elected U.S. president Bill Clinton to consider dropping the embargo, which one economic expert said only served to punish U.S. companies. For their part, the Vietnamese urged the lifting of these trade restrictions as well. On the streets of Saigon, T-shirts bearing the message "Lift the Embargo" worn by young Vietnamese anxious for economic development, became fashionable.

In 1993, the Clinton administration took the first step toward ending the embargo by allowing American companies to bid on development projects inside Vietnam. Now, for the first time since the Vietnam War era, Americans were able to visit Vietnam to conduct business. Further negotiations then occurred, resulting in Vietnam once again pledging to cooperate in the search for any Americans still listed as missing in action. In response to this renewed pledge, lingering opposition by political conservatives in the United States toward the normalization of relations with Vietnam gradually subsided. In early 1994, the Clinton administration dropped the nineteen-year-old American trade embargo altogether. U.S. companies then rushed to invest in Vietnam, as this 1994 news report observed:

> When President Clinton ended the U.S. trade embargo against Vietnam in early February, he might as well have fired a starter's pistol into the air. The race was joined. Within hours, Pepsi was giving away soda pop on the streets of Ho Chi Minh City . . . . Coca-Cola, Pepsi's chief competitor, immediately began shipping tons of its soft drinks into Vietnam from bottling plants throughout Southeast Asia. United Airlines announced it would begin flying into the country as soon as it got permission. Businessmen and women scrambled to get on already-scheduled flights to Hanoi and Ho Chi Minh City. "The stampede is on," said [an American investor].[88]

The lifting of the trade embargo was swiftly followed by a resumption of full diplomatic relations. In August 1995, for the first time in twenty years, the American flag was hoisted in Vietnam, flying atop the brand-new American embassy in Hanoi. In addition to achieving reconciliation with the United States, Vietnam also established fruitful diplomatic and economic relations with China and with countries in Western Europe, including France. Vietnam also joined several non-Communist governments in the Association of Southeast Asian Nations (ASEAN), an organization dedicated to promoting mutual economic growth.

Vietnam's new openness paid off. By 1996, foreign investment in the country had ballooned to $20 billion, with U.S. corporations investing over $1 billion.

Other countries with even larger investments in Vietnam included France, Taiwan, Hong Kong, Japan, and the Republic of Korea. By 1997, amid this robust business atmosphere, Vietnam's annual economic growth rate quadrupled to a remarkable 8 percent, becoming one of the fastest growing economies in the world. Inflation dropped below 4 percent, a far cry from the staggering 400 percent Vietnam had suffered from back in 1987.

FURTHER TROUBLES

Despite this apparent success, however, serious obstacles still stood in the way of sustained economic growth. For example, multinational companies eagerly trying to arrange business deals in Vietnam were constantly frustrated by a complex and confusing legal system in which written contracts were not enforceable, and new laws only confounded the problem. Irwin Jay Robinson, founder and president of the Vietnam-American Chamber of Commerce, observed, in Vietnam "they enact a new law and sometimes you don't know the text of it for weeks and months after it's enacted. When you finally find out what the law is, they may be amending it already because they've found it's impractical."[89] Often, Communist Party officials would enforce regulations in an arbitrary way. Bureaucratic red tape would delay the start of

projects and discourage some large companies from investing more money in Vietnam. The country developed a deserved reputation as a tough place to operate, as this news report revealed:

> Every investor [in Vietnam] has a different horror story. The paper that 3M imports to make Post-It Notes faces

A young woman sells bananas outside an American storefront. Vietnam's new economic openness has enabled foreign corporations to establish themselves there.

TEMPTATIONS AND CORRUPTIONS

Vietnam's economic openness under Doi Moi *brought new opportunities, but it also brought new temptations that served to worsen government corruption. David Lamb, an American reporter who covered the Vietnam War and returned to live there thirty years later, discusses this corruption in* Vietnam, Now.

"Vietnam's first generation of communist leaders—Ho Chi Minh, Pham Van Dong, Vo Nguyen Giap, and Le Duc Tho among others—came from scholarly backgrounds. Some of their fathers had served the emperors. Ho and his colleagues were seen as morally diligent, administratively efficient, incorruptible. . . . But the second generation that now ran Vietnam [from the late 1980s onward] encountered many temptations, with big money from donor groups and foreign investors floating around as a result of the government's Doi Moi open-door economic policy. Suddenly Vietnam was awash in corruption. It reached from the policeman on the beat to the high levels of government. There had always been perks involved with Party membership—better housing, better jobs, better educational opportunity for the elite's children, funded travel abroad—but now ordinary citizens knew they had to pay the traffic cop to avoid a ticket and bribe a low-paid civil servant to get something done at a ministry. Shopkeepers knew they had to pay to stay in business. Investors knew they had to pay to get a contract approved. In this new atmosphere, the leadership came to be viewed as cynical careerists; the Communist Party itself lost its mythical aura of wisdom and rectitude, which had enabled it to govern."

an arbitrarily high tariff as "office products" (40% duty) rather than "adhesive-backed paper" (10%). This makes it more expensive than the same Post-It Notes smugglers bring in from Thailand. Coca-Cola and Procter & Gamble both got into nasty public battles with insolvent [Vietnamese] joint-venture partners. . . . Cable and Wireless (C&W), a telecoms firm, spent five years trying to negotiate a

"roaming" agreement that would allow travelers to use their mobile phones in Vietnam. Virtually every country in Asia allowed this long ago (including even China and Cambodia). . . . [Eventually] C&W had enough; it abandoned a $207 million project to install 250,000 new lines in Hanoi. . . . Vietnam's charms are fading. This leaves it with a dilemma. If Vietnam persists in refusing to reform, it risks being left behind. But if it opens to foreigners, political change may become unstoppable.[90]

Many Vietnamese recognized the need to change the way their nation did business. Even legendary war leader General Vo Nguyen Giap admitted to Stanley Karnow, "There are two things that are just awful about this country: the bureaucracy and the corruption."[91] Making matters worse, Vietnam's state-controlled banking system was considered by Westerners to be unreliable. One could never be sure that deposited funds would actually be available for use, a major hindrance to daily business operations. In addition, inefficient state-owned factories, mismanaged and staffed by poorly motivated workers, were routinely given preferential treatment by Communist bureaucrats over foreign start-ups, soaking up valuable natural resources and labor while providing unprofitable results. These old-style Communist-run factories turned out poorly made, overpriced consumer products that paled in quality compared to imported goods.

By the late 1990s, these difficulties with doing business in Vietnam had combined with a sudden downturn in other Asian economies to bring Vietnam's economic growth to a screeching halt. As their own economies weakened, Japan, South Korea, and other countries scaled back business activities in Vietnam. As the flow of investment funds dried up, foreign-owned businesses throughout Vietnam closed and unemployment rose dramatically. The job losses hit particularly hard in the countryside, where many companies had built factories and where now up to 35 percent of the rural inhabitants remained chronically unemployed, except during harvest seasons.

Reacting to the steep economic downturn, various world leaders urged Vietnam to consider a whole new round of economic reforms. However, Vietnam's political leaders chose to ignore this advice out of fear that further reform would make an already-difficult situation even worse. Instead, they decided to follow a slower pace of reform and even to reverse some reforms that had previously been instituted after observing the effects of the financial crisis on neighboring countries. As one economic publication noted,

> The main effect of the Asian [financial] crisis was to confirm the leadership's suspicion that opening to the West invites disaster. After all, Indonesia and South Korea were knocked sideways [by the financial crisis] whereas isolated Vietnam was [comparatively] not much affected. [Vietnam's] leaders decided that slow economic growth was a price worth paying for stability. "They thought they had missed being hit by the bullet because they had not reformed enough to be a victim," observed Pete Peterson, the American ambassador.[92]

At the same time, Vietnam's leaders had also become increasingly concerned about the erosion of their own influence since they had opened the door to foreigners. Bit by bit they were losing control over a youthful population that seemed eager to adopt new ideas and values from America and elsewhere. Reacting to this, Vietnam's leaders decided to reestablish some control over their society by turning back the clock a bit, using their considerable powers to crack down on political dissent and stifle free expression.

STRIVING FOR CONTROL

During the early 1990s, Vietnam's political leaders had watched with apprehension as one country after another in Eastern Europe converted virtually overnight from communism to capitalism following mass demonstrations on the part of their people for political reform. To prevent this from happening in Vietnam, hundreds of people were arrested as a precautionary measure on the premise that their contact with people from the West made them likely to agitate for political reform.

An updated constitution, enacted in 1992, reaffirmed the dominance of the Communist Party, stating, "The Communist Party of Vietnam, the vanguard of the Vietnamese working class, the faithful representative of the rights and interests of the working class, the toiling people, and the whole nation, acting upon the Marxist-Leninist doctrine and Ho Chi Minh's thought, is the force leading the State and society." Such efforts to forestall changes in the nation's political system did not, however, keep Vietnam's

East German soldiers kick down a portion of the Berlin Wall in 1989. Its fall and the defeat of communism throughout Eastern Europe prompted Vietnam to limit its citizens' contact with the Western world.

CHILDREN IN DESPAIR

At the dawn of the twenty-first century, thousands of children were homeless in Vietnam living in despair and misery. As quoted by Knight-Ridder/Tribune News Service, Gregg Jones of the *Dallas Morning News* writes, "Hanoi has an estimated five thousand street children, who can earn two to three times as much as their poor parents in the countryside by shining shoes or begging on city streets. The problem is even worse in Ho Chi Minh City, the former Saigon, where there are an estimated seven thousand children." Reporters David Liebhold and Huw Watkin, writing in *Time International*, report that at Nha Trang, a popular tourist resort, homeless children as young as seven years old sleep on the beach and try to feed themselves by selling chewing gum, doughnuts, or T-shirts.

Without families to protect them, these children get shaken down by thugs. Many also fall victim to Western pedophiles. Liebhold and Watkin quoted Kim Le, a Vietnamese-Canadian who returned to Vietnam in 1996 and now manages a small bar in Nha Trang, as saying, "The Government doesn't know how to handle the problem, so they're just ignoring it." After she caught a German tourist molesting a ten-year-old boy in a hotel, Kim Le wrote a letter to the government and local authorities—to no effect. "To get the police to do something is impossible. They say, 'There's no proof, so we can't do anything.'"

Sexual abuse of children by foreigners is not as widespread in Vietnam as it is in nearby Cambodia, Thailand, or the Philippines. But as authorities crack down elsewhere, pedophiles are choosing Vietnam as a safer option. Faced with official inaction, Kim Le began printing T-shirts with messages saying "Child Sex Is a Crime" and handing them out on the beach. Over the past three years, she has distributed thousands of T-shirts and printed flyers to raise awareness. The children believe it helps deter the pedophiles. "When they see the T-shirts, they get scared," said one boy who was sexually abused. But the problem remains. "Hundreds of kids are living in fear and shame," Kim Le said. "Who's going to take care of them?"

leaders from attempting to reignite economic growth, as also noted in the new constitution: "The aim of the State's economic policy is to make the people rich and the country strong. . . . The State encourages foreign organizations and individuals to invest funds and technologies in Vietnam."[93]

As much as they desired Western capital to help build Vietnam, the country's leaders feared the consequences of Western influence in Vietnamese society. As a result, the government launched repeated propaganda campaigns denouncing what it called "social evils" and "spiritual pollution," targeting prostitution, drug use, pornographic and violent videos, gambling, pop music, and street signs featuring foreign advertisements.

Police raids often accompanied these propaganda campaigns. These actions were undertaken, as one Communist official explained, "to keep things safe and clean for the country."[94] One such raid in February 1996 began by targeting outdoor advertisements, including Coca-Cola and Kodak, along with local shop signs printed in English, all of which were covered with a fresh coat of white paint. Next to be raided were video rental stores, music stores, kararoke bars, and a dance hall. After the raid, an old-fashioned patriotic parade was staged featuring the presence of flag-waving children and local Communist officials.

However, such campaigns were only modestly successful. In particular, most young urban Vietnamese had become accustomed to ignoring state propaganda with its stodgy, conformist messages. Former news correspondent Robert Templer, who visited Saigon, noted, "'Social evils' campaigns play well to a fairly small and aging group shocked by what they see as a society in decline, but they have little appeal to a growing urban middle class that is young, individualistic and increasingly driven by [Western-style] consumption."[95] Over time, the various social evils would all reappear on the streets of Saigon and elsewhere, lasting until the next cycle of propaganda and police raids.

By 1997, government authorities faced a new and even greater challenge in coping with the spread of AIDS in Vietnam among prostitutes and intravenous drug users. By 1997, over five thousand people had tested positive, forcing the govern-ment to make an attempt to educate those at risk about the dangers of HIV/AIDS. But here, too, the government failed to have a significant impact because of its reliance on outmoded heavy-handed tactics, including cartoonlike scare posters, political-style rallies, and door-to-door visits by dour party officials. To Vietnam's trendy urban youth, the AIDS information campaign seemed like the usual party propaganda and was therefore mainly ignored.

REBELLIOUS YOUTH

The failure of the nation's anti-AIDS campaign highlights the reality that Vietnam is a very young country. In fact, half of Vietnam's population of 80 million people was born after 1975, when the fall of South Vietnam to the north's Communists occurred. Therefore, they have no firsthand knowledge of the American war and have little appreciation of North Vietnam's long revolutionary struggle. Like young people everywhere, they want to have fun and are greatly attracted to American-style pop culture and consumerism. This is especially noticeable in Ho Chi Minh City (which most Vietnamese still refer to as Saigon), where the freewheeling attitudes of pre-Communist days have slowly reemerged. Former news reporter Arnold Issacs described the rowdy atmosphere that has prevailed despite government efforts to crack down:

On Saigon's crowded streets, hustlers, hawkers, prostitutes, destitute war veterans, and homeless children mingled under splashy, colorful advertisements for credit cards and video recorders. Commercial billboards overshadowed the old black-and-white photographs of Ho Chi Minh and the revolutionary slogans lettered on fading street corner banners. . . .Youthful crowds in the latest American-style fashions crowded into nightclubs where deafening rock music pounded from loudspeakers into hot, smoky nights. . . .These children of a new commercial elite lived by the watchword phrase *song voi*—"living quickly."[96]

In both Saigon and Hanoi, a typical weekend often saw high-speed motorbike races during the predawn hours, with dozens of young racers roaring wildly through the streets and crowds of youthful onlookers cheering the pandemonium. Over time, the races developed into a kind of organized sport involving gambling and prize money. "I loved the speed and freedom,"[97] said one twenty-two-year-old former racer.

The older generation that fought to unify Vietnam watched with dismay as their offspring displayed little interest in politics and on occasion expressed open disdain for communism, the foundation of Vietnam's government. In earlier times, especially in the north, Vietnamese youth would have had a completely different perspective. During three decades of warfare, there was an overwhelming emphasis on duty, obligation, youthful sacrifice, and martyrdom. Unlike their dutiful parents, however, Vietnam's postwar youth

A downtown Hanoi street crowded with motorbikes illustrates Vietnam's embrace of a faster-paced, more modern lifestyle.

came of age much more self-centered, interested in personal achievement and the pursuit of money and leisure instead of state-ordered unselfishness. According to a 2000 *Time International* magazine report,

Children of one of the starkest generation gaps in the world, [Vietnamese youth] have no interest in hearing about the hardships their parents endured in the fighting that ended a quarter century ago. They are determined to get on with their own lives, to make up for lost time since the communists took over and dumped Vietnam at the bottom of Asia's economic league. Theirs is a world of mobile phones, mopeds, long days at work and long evenings dating in coffee shops.[98]

With their bolder attitudes, Vietnam's youth are also not afraid to voice honest opinions about perceived economic and social injustices, and this causes the government great concern. This new attitude also causes tension at home. "My friends quarrel with their parents, because they're different from their parents in every way,"[99] said a nineteen-year-old college student in Saigon.

To many older people, Vietnam appears to be in danger of losing its roots. The country's long revolutionary history is today all but ignored by pleasure-seeking young people. In a revealing survey taken in the mid-1990s, eighteen hundred young people were presented with a few names of important heroic figures from Vietnam's past but in most cases could not recognize them. However, more than 85 percent easily recognized the name of American pop singer Michael Jackson

and a popular football star from Argentina. Journalist Robert Templer notes:

The state no longer controls ideas about what it is to be heroic. While the [official] Vietnamese media still hark on about security and national independence, central aspects of the Communist Party's legitimacy, the subject arouses little interest among the young; asked what they cared about in a poll, only 20 percent said the nation's security, the least important item on a list of twelve. Work, economic status, education and [government] corruption all ranked significantly higher.[100]

Television has emerged as a major influence in the lives of Vietnam's young people. Over 80 percent of Vietnamese are avid TV watchers, often bypassing state-controlled channels via illegal satellite dishes that pick up foreign programming, including CNN and STAR-TV, a Hong Kong–based satellite network. Vietnam's youth, eager to be hip, often imitate the behavior seen in martial arts and gangster movies—to the dismay of Communist officials as well as parents. "Children today see the bad actions on TV and they act the same," said one mother of two teenage boys in Saigon. "We have fighting, violence, disrespect. All parents now worry about TV." Her fourteen-year-old son, however, had a somewhat different perspective: "When we see the world on TV, we know we are behind. Now, we want to catch up."[101]

Vietnam's Communist leaders have thus far failed to stop their power and influence from eroding as foreign ideas and consumer values from America, Western

FEARING THE INTERNET

The Internet with its free flow of ideas worries Vietnam's Communist officials, who feel it may serve to undermine their authority. As a result, they have enforced strict censorship policies. In 1996, even before Vietnam was connected to the Internet, the Communists announced regulations forbidding "data that can affect national security, social order, and safety, or information that is not appropriate to the culture, morality, and traditional customs of the Vietnamese people, "as reported on CNETNews.com at the time.

As of June 2002, there were only 175,000 registered Internet users in Vietnam, according to Nandotimes.com. However, the actual number of people with online access, mainly through Vietnam's four thousand or so new Internet cafés, is estimated to be up to 600,000. Most users are students between the ages of fourteen and twenty-four. According to the website Vnunet.com, about 70 percent use the Internet for chatting, 10 percent for games, and 10 percent for e-mail. Only 10 percent actually surf websites, but half of these have reportedly accessed sites with antigovernment or pornographic content.

In the summer of 2002, Communist officials announced they they would crack down on people accessing "poisonous and harmful" information. One of Vietnam's most popular websites, ttvnonline.com, was shut down amid charges that it violated press laws and "distorted the truth." Cyber-dissident Le Chi Quang, a Vietnamese writer, was arrested because of articles he wrote and posted on the Internet that were critical of the Communist regime. Pham Hong Son, marketing director of a pharmaceutical company, was also arrested for translating and circulating an article on democracy taken from the U.S. State Department's website.

Europe, and other Asian countries continue flooding into the country, captivating young minds. The dreary old Communist Party propaganda attacking Western-style consumerism as unpatriotic is laughed at by a youthful population that has an overwhelming desire to be rich. As one American reporter noted during a visit to Saigon in 2000, "'VC' in this commercial hub—where half the population wasn't yet born in 1968—[now] stands for venture capitalist, not Viet Cong."[102]

Although members of Vietnam's older generation may view their offspring with apprehension and even alarm, in reality Vietnam's young people exhibit some strong positive qualities. Whatever their motivation, they are driven to succeed and are willing to work long hours. They yearn for self-improvement and apply themselves with zeal whenever the opportunity for economic advancement arises. But as the older generation passes away and the mantle of power shifts to the young, they will have to overcome a daunting array of social and economic problems that have been handed down to them in order to uplift their country, including a pay-as-you-go education system that has fallen into complete disarray.

HUNGRY TO LEARN

By the mid-1990s, Vietnam had 40 million people under the age of twenty-five. The country's schools were simply unable to accommodate so many students and suffered a notable decline in quality. There was a severe shortage of qualified teachers; more than 100,000 additional teachers were needed to cope with the vast numbers of students. In many towns, insufficient classroom space required young students to attend classes in shifts. A scarcity of books and science materials only added to the problem.

Despite the bad conditions, Vietnam's struggling teachers often encounter young students hungry to learn. Charles Miller, a teacher from the United States, observed one such scene at Catdang, a two-thousand-person rice-farming hamlet in northern Vietnam:

Young people comprise a high percentage of Vietnamese society. A decrease in government spending for education has led to higher rates of juvenile illiteracy, crime, and prostitution.

I was teaching English in a very standard American high school in a suburb of Tokyo and I got a chance to take a three-week vacation. I walked into this school in Catdang, into this classroom, and the man who was teaching had no shoes on. The kids had no pens, no notebooks. There was no chalk or blackboard, no writing tools or textbooks. He was teaching geometry, and the kids—there were about 40 of them, 36 or so boys and four girls—were riveted by what he was saying. Imagine, a group of 13- and 14-year-olds sitting absolutely still, preparing for a test to get into high school. The room had no lights, no windows, just holes cut out of the brick walls of the building.[103]

To make matters worse, government spending on education actually declined nearly 20 percent in the late 1990s. In the countryside, many Vietnamese parents, required like all parents to pay for schooling, could not afford the bill, forcing their children to drop out. Up to 70 percent of young students in rural areas were unable to attend high school and instead took their chances at finding jobs to support themselves and aid their struggling families. Each year, more than 1 million of these poorly educated, ill-prepared young people regularly joined an already overcrowded job market. Unable to find work, vast numbers of these youths in Saigon and other cities idled away their time entertaining themselves with rock videos, martial arts movies, and other nonproductive pursuits. Not surprisingly, a notable increase in reports of juveniles being involved in robbery, assault, and prostitution occurred.

While large numbers of Vietnamese youth remain miserably unemployed, at the top of the heap, better-off middle-class and college-educated Vietnamese, not much older than themselves, enjoy splendid lifestyles. These children of successful businesspeople and influential party officials have motorbikes, pagers, cellphones, personal stereos, and trendy clothing to wear. In addition, the offspring of high-ranking government officials routinely enjoy much better opportunities and have an easier time climbing the ladder of success. And they are not shy about showing off their good fortune.

Wherever they travel, however, these flashy show-offs are greeted by the envious stares of unhappy youths who would like to enjoy the same things but have little real hope of ever doing so. Jealousy, frustration, and anger have thus caused serious tensions to appear between Vietnam's emerging social classes—in a socialist society that in theory is supposed to be classless.

Vietnam's future leaders will have to cope with the growing antagonism between the majority "have-nots" and the few privileged "haves" to keep the country politically stable. "A gap between rich and poor can lead to instability,"[104] admitted a high-ranking Communist official in 2000.

WIDE OPEN FUTURE

Since the fall of Saigon and the reunification of Vietnam, the country has undergone enormous changes, mainly by necessity. Faced with a failed economy, Vietnam evolved from an isolationist hard-nosed Communist economy into a

Parade goers hold pictures of Ho Chi Minh to commemorate the twenty-fifth anniversary of the Vietnam War's end.

hybrid political system, part socialist, part capitalist. It has also opened itself to the outside world. Nations such as the United States, France, and China, which once sent troops to battle perceived enemies, now send economic aid and look for investment opportunities.

With the passage of time, all of the aging Communist revolutionaries who fought so long for independence and struggled to administer the awkward peace that followed will fade from the scene. Into their place will step a new generation that has already demonstrated that it cares more about economic security than political ideology. Where this might lead politically no one can predict for sure, but it appears likely that Vietnam will edge further away from its Communist roots.

Despite the political uncertainty, there are many reasons to be optimistic about Vietnam's uncharted journey into the new millennium. With its 80 million inhabitants, abundant natural resources, and so many eager young minds thirsting for knowledge, Vietnam may indeed be on the verge of unparalleled success. Since reunification, the biggest hindrance preventing Vietnam's hardworking, dependable people from moving the country forward has been the government itself. With new leadership, the government's inherent corruption and bureaucratic stubbornness might over time give way to innovation and youthful spontaneity—the spark that might ignite the potential of an entire nation.

Notes

Introduction: Centuries of Strife

1. Quoted in Stanley Karnow, *Vietnam: A History*. New York: Penguin Books, 1997, p. 119.

2. Quoted in The History Place, "United States in Vietnam, 1945–1975: Seeds of Conflict," 1999. www.historyplace.com.

3. Quoted in Judith Vecchione, writer-producer, *Vietnam: A Television History*. Boston: WGBH-TV, 1983.

4. Quoted in Karnow, *Vietnam*, p. 71.

Chapter 1: The American War

5. Quoted in Ian McLeod, producer, *Vietnam: The Ten Thousand Day War*. Toronto: Canadian Broadcasting Corporation, 1980.

6. Quoted in David Chanoff and Doan Van Toai, *Portrait of the Enemy: The Other Side of the Vietnam War, Told Through Interviews with North Vietnamese, Former Vietcong, and Southern Opposition Leaders*. New York: Random House, 1986, p. 169.

7. Quoted in Vecchione, *Vietnam*.

8. Michael Lee Lanning and Dan Cragg, *Inside the VC and the NVA: The Real Story of North Vietnam's Armed Forces*. New York: Fawcett Columbine, 1992, p. 164.

9. Quoted in Vecchione, *Vietnam*.

10. Quoted in Gil Dorland, *Legacy of Discord: Voices of the Vietnam War Era*. Washington, DC: Brassey's, 2001, p. 204.

11. Quoted in McLeod, *Vietnam*.

12. Quoted in Vecchione, *Vietnam*.

13. Quoted in John Clark Pratt, comp., *Vietnam Voices: Perspectives on the War Years, 1941–1982*. New York: Penguin Books, 1984, p. 254.

14. Quoted in Pratt, *Vietnam Voices*, p. 256.

15. Quoted in Marvin E. Gettleman, H. Bruce Franklin, Jane Franklin, and Marilyn B. Young, eds., *Vietnam and America: The Most Comprehensive Documented History of the Vietnam War*. New York: Grove Press, 1995, pp. 312–15.

16. Quoted in McLeod, *Vietnam*.

17. Quoted in McLeod, *Vietnam*.

18. Quoted in McLeod, *Vietnam*.

19. Peter Scholl-Latour, *Death in the Rice Fields: An Eyewitness Account of Vietnam's Three Wars, 1945–1979*. New York: St. Martin's Press, 1979, p. 139.

20. Quoted in *Reporting Vietnam*, vol. 1: *American Journalism, 1959–1969*. New York: Library of America, 1998, p. 581.

21. Quoted in McLeod, *Vietnam*.

22. Quoted in Gettleman et al., *Vietnam and America*, p. 409.

23. Quoted in McLeod, *Vietnam*.

24. Quoted in McLeod, *Vietnam*.

Chapter 2: America Withdraws

25. Quoted in *Reporting Vietnam*, vol. 2: *American Journalism 1969–1975*. New York: Library of America, 1998, p. 233.

26. Quoted in Dorland, *Legacy of Discord*, p. 208.

27. Quoted in Dorland, *Legacy of Discord*, p. 208.

28. Quoted in The History Place, "United States in Vietnam, 1945–1975: The Bitter End," 1999. www.historyplace.com.

29. Quoted in McLeod, *Vietnam*.

30. Quoted in The History Place, "United States in Vietnam, 1945–1975: The Bitter End."

31. Quoted in David Fulghum et al., *The Vietnam Experience: South Vietnam on Trial.* Boston: Boston Publishing, 1985, p. 64.

32. Quoted in The History Place, "United States in Vietnam, 1945–1975: The Bitter End."

33. Quoted in Karnow, *Vietnam*, p. 666.

34. Quoted in McLeod, *Vietnam*.

35. Quoted in Dorland, *Legacy of Discord*, p. 211.

36. Quoted in Al Santoli, ed., *Everything We Had: An Oral History of the Vietnam War by Thirty-Three American Soldiers Who Fought It.* New York: Ballantine Books, 1981, pp. 176–77.

37. Quoted in Fulghum et al., *The Vietnam Experience*, p. 57.

38. Quoted in Dorland, *Legacy of Discord*, p. 209.

Chapter 3: South Vietnam Collapses

39. Quoted in Larry Engelmann, *Tears Before the Rain: An Oral History of the Fall of South Vietnam.* New York: Oxford University Press, 1990, p. 302.

40. Quoted in Edward Doyle et al., *The Vietnam Experience: The Aftermath.* Boston: Boston Publishing, 1985, p. 22.

41. Quoted in Engelmann, *Tears Before the Rain*, p. 302.

42. Quoted in Dorland, *Legacy of Discord*, p. 144.

43. Quoted in Tim Page and John Pimlott, *Nam: The Vietnam Experience, 1965–75.* New York: Barnes & Noble Books, 1995, p. 547.

44. Quoted in Engelmann, *Tears Before the Rain*, p. 241.

45. Quoted in Page and Pimlott, *Nam*, p. 548.

46. Peter Scholl-Latour, *Death in the Rice Fields*, p. 220.

47. Quoted in Engelmann, *Tears Before the Rain*, pp. 4–5.

48. Quoted in Doyle et al., *The Vietnam Experience: The Aftermath*, p. 28.

49. Quoted in Doyle et al., *The Vietnam Experience: The Aftermath*, p. 31.

50. Quoted in Doyle et al., *The Vietnam Experience: The Aftermath*, p. 31.

51. Quoted in Harry G. Summers, *Historical Atlas of the Vietnam War.* Boston: Houghton Mifflin, 1995, p. 202.

52. Quoted in The History Place, "United States in Vietnam, 1945–1975: The Bitter End."

53. Quoted in Page and Pimlott, *Nam*, p. 551.

54. Quoted in Engelmann, *Tears Before the Rain*, p. 127.

55. Quoted in Page and Pimlott, *Nam*, p. 559.

56. Quoted in Engelmann, *Tears Before the Rain*, p. 300.

57. Quoted in Page and Pimlott, *Nam*, p. 558.

Chapter 4: The Communists Take Over

58. Quoted in Edward Doyle et al., *The Vietnam Experience: The Aftermath*, p. 8.

59. Quoted in John S. Bowman, ed., *The World Almanac of the Vietnam War.* New York: Pharos Books, 1986, p. 345.

60. Quoted in David Chanoff and Doan Van Toai, *The Vietnamese Gulag: A Revolution Betrayed.* New York: Simon & Schuster, 1986, p. 187.

61. Quoted in Doyle et al., *The Vietnam Experience: The Aftermath*, p. 15.

62. Quoted in Doyle et al., *The Vietnam Experience: The Aftermath*, p. 17.

63. Quoted in Dorland, *Legacy of Discord*, p. 147.

64. Quoted in Engelmann, *Tears Before the Rain*, p. 239.

65. Quoted in Engelmann, *Tears Before the Rain*, p. 336.

Chapter 5: The Boat People

66. Quoted in John Tenhula, *Voices from Southeast Asia.* New York: Holmes & Meier, 1991, pp. 64–65.

67. Quoted in Engelmann, *Tears Before the Rain*, p. 332.

68. Quoted in Tenhula, *Voices from Southeast Asia*, p. 69.

69. Quoted in Peter Vilbig, "The New Rebels," *New York Times Upfront*, January 1, 2001.

70. Quoted in Doyle et al., *The Vietnam Experience: The Aftermath*, p. 40.

71. Quoted in Doyle et al., *The Vietnam Experience: The Aftermath*, p. 55.

72. Quoted in Engelmann, *Tears Before the Rain*, p. 270.

73. Michael P. Smith and Bernadette Tarallo, "The Unsettling Resettlement of Vietnamese Boat People," *USA Today* magazine, March 1993, p. 27.

74. Mike Tharp, "Divided by Generations: Little Saigon: Vietnamese-Americans Form Community in Westminster, California," *U.S. News & World Report*, July 17, 2000, p. 42.

75. *The Economist*, "Their Bonnie Lies over the Ocean," April 27, 1991, p. A29.

Chapter 6: Vietnam Takes Cambodia

76. Quoted in Ben Kiernan, *The Pol Pot Regime*. New Haven, CT: Yale University Press, 1996, p. 44.

77. Quoted in Doyle et al., *The Vietnam Experience: The Aftermath*, p. 54.

78. Quoted in Dith Pran, comp., *Children of Cambodia's Killing Fields*. New Haven, CT: Yale University Press, 1997, pp. 22–23.

79. Quoted in Doyle et al., *The Vietnam Experience: The Aftermath*, p. 64.

80. Quoted in Doyle et al., *The Vietnam Experience: The Aftermath*, p. 58.

81. Quoted in Tenhula, *Voices from Southeast Asia*, p. 71.

82. Quoted in Doyle et al., *The Vietnam Experience: The Aftermath*, p. 87.

83. Robert Kaylor, "At the Scene: How Guerillas Pin Down a Soviet Ally," *U.S. News & World Report*, August 8, 1983, p. 25.

84. Stewart Powell, Robert S. Dudney, and Robert Kaylor, "Vietnam: The Lasting Impact," *U.S. News & World Report*, April 22, 1985, p. 35.

85. Donald Kirk, "Vietnam Looks to the West," *New Leader*, July 25, 1988, p. 7.

Chapter 7: New Problems, Old Solutions

86. Quoted in Arnold R. Issacs, *Vietnam Shadows: The War, Its Ghosts, and Its Legacy*. Baltimore: Johns Hopkins University Press, 1997, p. 166.

87. Colin Leinster, "Vietnam Revisited: Turn to the Right?" *Fortune*, August 1, 1988, p. 84.

88. Terry McDermott, "Dollars, Memories Lure U.S. Businessmen to Vietnam," Knight-Ridder/Tribune News Service, February 14, 1994.

89. Quoted in Jason Goldberg, "Is 'Doi Moi' a Business Ploy?" *Insight on the News*, March 14, 1994, p. 34.

90. *The Economist*, "Goodnight, Vietnam," January 8, 2000, p. 65.

91. Quoted in Allan E. Goodman, "Vietnam in 1995: It Was a Very Good Year," *Washington Quarterly*, Spring 1996, p. 137.

92. *The Economist*, "Goodnight, Vietnam."

93. *Constitution of the Socialist Republic of Vietnam*, Chapter Two: Economic System; Article 16, Article 25, as found at the website of the Embassy of the Socialist Republic of Vietnam in the U.S., www.vietnamembassy-usa.org.

94. Quoted in Kristin Huckshorn, "Vietnamese Government Begins Crackdown on 'Social Evils,'" Knight-Ridder/Tribune News Service, January 31, 1996.

95. Robert Templer, *Shadows and Wind: A View of Modern Vietnam*. New York: Penguin Books, 1998, p. 231.

96. Issacs, *Vietnam Shadows*, p. 180.

97. Quoted in Issacs, *Vietnam Shadows*, p. 331.

98. *Time International*, "The Kids Are All Right," August 21, 2000, p. 76.

99. Quoted in Vilbig, "The New Rebels."

100. Templer, *Shadows and Wind*, p. 342.

101. Quoted in Kristin Huckshorn, "Many Viets Link TV to Delinquency," Knight-Ridder/Tribune News Service, March 28, 1996.

102. "Saigon 25 Years After the Fall," *Fortune*, May 1, 2000, p. 208.

103. Quoted in Eleanor J. Bader, "Catdang Basket Project: A Vietnam Story," *Dollars & Sense*, July/August 1997, p. 32.

104. Quoted in *The Economist*, "Bye-Bye, Uncle Ho," November 11, 2000, p. 31.

For Further Reading

Bernard Edelman, ed., *Dear America: Letters Home from Vietnam.* New York: W.W. Norton, 1985. One of the most interesting books published on the war, this compelling collection of letters and poems reveals the personal side of those who served.

David Lamb, *Vietnam, Now.* New York: PublicAffairs, 2002. Three decades after he covered the war as a combat correspondent, Lamb returned to Vietnam and discovered the richness of a people he hardly got to know during the war.

Bill McCloud, *What Should We Tell Our Children About Vietnam?* Norman: University of Oklahoma Press, 1989. Ideal for young students, this is a collection of 128 short responses to the title's meaningful question from veterans, writers, and public figures of the Vietnam War era.

Tim Page and John Pimlott, *Nam: The Vietnam Experience, 1965–75.* New York: Barnes & Noble Books, 1995. A well-balanced book with an emphasis on photos and graphics. Particularly relevant is that perspectives are given by contributors from all sides, including the press, the VC, and the NVA.

Tricia Springstubb, *The Vietnamese Americans.* San Diego: Lucent Books, 2002. This book examines the background of events leading up to the exodus from Vietnam and explores the many challenges faced by Vietnamese building new lives in the United States.

Spencer C. Tucker, ed., *The Encyclopedia of the Vietnam War.* Oxford: Oxford University Press, 1998. An excellent guide for students concerning the multitude of terms, places, and people involved in the war.

Works Consulted

Books

Christian G. Appy, *Working Class War.* Chapel Hill: University of North Carolina Press, 1993. Explores the experiences and attitudes of the 2.5 million Americans who served in Vietnam, painting a compelling portrait of the war as it was lived by the troops.

Mark Baker, ed., *Nam: The Vietnam War in the Words of the Men and Women Who Fought There.* New York: Cooper Square Press, 1981. Contains firsthand interviews with numerous military personnel who served in the war.

John S. Bowman, ed., *The World Almanac of the Vietnam War.* New York: Pharos Books, 1986. A well-balanced book in almanac form that covers places and chronological events. There are many charts, maps, and significant pictures to support the information.

David Chanoff and Doan Van Toai, *Portrait of the Enemy: The Other Side of the Vietnam War, Told Through Interviews with North Vietnamese, Former Vietcong, and Southern Opposition Leaders.* New York: Random House, 1986. The fascinating personal narratives in this book challenge some widely held assumptions about both the political and military aspect of America's involvement in Vietnam.

Joan D. Criddle and Teeda Butt Mam, *To Destroy You Is No Loss: The Odyssey of a Cambodian Family.* New York: Doubleday, 1987. A heart-wrenching account of daily life amid the unending nightmare of Pol Pot's genocidal regime.

Dith Pran, comp., *Children of Cambodia's Killing Fields.* New Haven, CT: Yale University Press, 1997. An extraordinary compilation of true stories providing a child's-eye look at life under the murderous Pol Pot regime.

Doan Van Toai and David Chanoff, *The Vietnamese Gulag: A Revolution Betrayed.* New York: Simon & Schuster, 1986. An informative book on South Vietnam's transformation into a highly regimented Communist dictatorship.

Gil Dorland, *Legacy of Discord: Voices of the Vietnam War Era.* Washington, DC: Brassey's, 2001. Assembled by the author from interviews with a cross-section of notable individuals from the Vietnam War era, including Henry Kissinger, William Westmoreland, David Halberstam, and Tom Hayden, among others.

Clark Dougan et al., *The Vietnam Experience: The Fall of the South.* Boston: Boston Publishing, 1985. A detailed examination of South Vietnam's rapid demise in 1975 as the North Vietnamese invaded.

Edward Doyle et al., *The Vietnam Experience: The Aftermath.* Boston: Boston Publishing, 1985. Chronicles events in

Vietnam and Cambodia from 1975 to 1985, including the Communists' unification of Vietnam and the actions of the Pol Pot regime in Cambodia.

Larry Engelmann, *Tears Before the Rain: An Oral History of the Fall of South Vietnam.* New York: Oxford University Press, 1990. Presents the testimony of seventy eyewitnesses, including students, TV media figures, Vietnamese generals, pilots, and numerous others, to provide a harrowing, firsthand account of the fall of Saigon.

Bernard B. Fall, ed., *Ho Chi Minh on Revolution: Selected Writings, 1920–66.* New York: Praeger, 1967. A fascinating collection of letters and speeches by North Vietnam's revolutionary leader.

David Fulghum et al., *The Vietnam Experience: South Vietnam on Trial.* Boston: Boston Publishing, 1985. Covers events from mid-1970 to 1972, including Vietnamization and the north's Easter Offensive.

Marvin E. Gettleman, H. Bruce Franklin, Jane Franklin, and Marilyn B. Young, eds., *Vietnam and America: The Most Comprehensive Documented History of the Vietnam War.* New York: Grove Press, 1995. This complete history of the Vietnam War, as documented in essays by leading experts and in original source material, illuminates both sides of America's encounter with Vietnam.

Arnold R. Issacs, *Vietnam Shadows: The War, Its Ghosts, and Its Legacy.* Baltimore: Johns Hopkins University Press, 1997. The former war correspondent examines Vietnam in the decades after the fall of Saigon.

Stanley Karnow, *Vietnam: A History.* New York: Penguin Books, 1997. The Pulitzer Prize–winning account of the war that clarifies, analyzes, and demystifies the tragic ordeal; filled with fresh revelations drawn from secret documents and from exclusive interviews with the participants.

Ben Kiernan, *The Pol Pot Regime.* New Haven, CT: Yale University Press, 1996. The first scholarly study of the Cambodian genocide, drawn from more than five hundred interviews by the author and from his examination of previously unexplored archives.

Michael Lee Lanning and Dan Cragg, *Inside the VC and the NVA: The Real Story of North Vietnam's Armed Forces.* New York: Fawcett Colombine, 1992. A look at the other side, compiled by two Vietnam veterans from twenty-six hundred interviews with VC/NVA, POWs, and defectors.

Someth May, *Cambodian Witness.* New York: Random House, 1986. An autobiography exploring one family's ordeal as Cambodia changed overnight from a relatively peaceful society into a place of unremitting terror.

Military History Institute of Vietnam, *Victory in Vietnam: The Official History of the People's Army of Vietnam, 1954–1975,* Merle L. Pribbenow, trans. Lawrence: University Press of Kansas, 2002. This new release contains a wealth of detailed military information provided by the Communists themselves concerning battlefield maneuvers and various strategies they used to win, along with an obligatory dose of self-serving propaganda.

Richard Nixon, *No More Vietnams*. New York: Arbor House, 1985. Nixon's own personal analysis of what went wrong in Vietnam and how the United States can avoid making the same mistakes in the future.

John Clark Pratt, comp., *Vietnam Voices: Perspectives in the War Years, 1941–1982*. New York: Penguin Books, 1984. A chronological arrangement of oral and written documentation presenting viewpoints on Vietnam's wars from the various nationalities involved, including North and South Vietnamese, Americans, French, Cambodians, and more.

Reporting Vietnam: American Journalism, 1959–1975. 2 vols. New York: Library of America, 1998. A compilation of excellent combat-front writing by famous journalists such as David Halberstam, Bernard Fall, Neil Sheehan, and others. Vol. 1 covers reports from 1959–1969. Vol. 2 includes reports from 1969–1975.

Al Santoli, ed., *Everything We Had: An Oral History of the Vietnam War by Thirty-Three American Soldiers Who Fought It*. New York: Ballantine Books, 1981. A powerful account of the Vietnam War by combat soldiers, compiled by a combat veteran; the ex-periences and insight ring true for soldiers who have seen hostile fire in any conflict.

Peter Scholl-Latour, *Death in the Rice Fields: An Eyewitness Account of Vietnam's Three Wars, 1945–1979*. New York: St. Martin's Press, 1979. Journalist Peter Scholl-Latour was present in Vietnam from the French intervention through the American war and also observed China's brief invasion.

Gerald S. Strober and Deborah Hart Strober, *Nixon: An Oral History of His Presidency*. New York: HarperCollins, 1994. Contains more than a hundred candid interviews of people's opinions on everything from Vietnam to Watergate.

Harry G. Summers, *Historical Atlas of the Vietnam War*. Boston: Houghton Mifflin, 1995. Color maps and photos provide a visual analysis of the war, with text based on both U.S. and Vietnamese postwar accounts.

Robert Templer, *Shadows and Wind: A View of Modern Vietnam*. New York: Penguin Books, 1998. Templer profiles the postwar economic and cultural policies in Vietnam.

John Tenhula, *Voices from Southeast Asia*. New York: Holmes & Meier, 1991. Seventy-five refugees from Southeast Asia recall their harrowing experiences and the challenges they faced in adapting to their new home in America.

Truong Nhu Tang. *A Vietcong Memoir: An Inside Account of the Vietnam War and Its Aftermath*. New York: Harcourt

Brace Jovanovich, 1985. A rare glimpse into daily life among the Viet Cong and the disillusionment that many experienced following reunification.

Periodicals

Eleanor J. Bader, "Catdang Basket Project: A Vietnam Story," *Dollars & Sense*, July/August 1997.

George J. Church, "Saigon: The Final Ten Days." *Time*, April 24, 1995.

The Economist, "Bye-Bye, Uncle Ho," November 11, 2000.

———, "Goodnight, Vietnam," January 8, 2000.

———, "Their Bonnie Lies over the Ocean," April 27, 1991.

Fortune, "Saigon Twenty-five Years After the Fall," May 1, 2000.

Jason Goldberg, "Is 'Doi Moi' a Business Ploy?" *Insight on the News*, March 14, 1994.

Allan E. Goodman, "Vietnam in 1995: It Was a Very Good Year," *Washington Quarterly*, Spring 1996.

Kristin Huckshorn, "Many Viets Link TV to Delinquency," Knight-Ridder/Tribune News Service, March 28, 1996.

Gregg Jones, "Leaders Slow to Accept Change, but Many Vietnamese Embrace It," Knight-Ridder/Tribune News Service, April 28, 2002.

———, "Vietnamese Government Begins Crackdown on 'Social Evils,'" Knight-Ridder/Tribune News Service, January 31, 1996.

———, "Vietnamese Hunt Their Own MIAs—150,000 of Them" Knight-Ridder/Tribune News Service, August 2, 1995.

Stanley Karnow, "Lost Inside the Machine: A Historian Describes the Paranoia of Soldiers Trapped in an Unwinnable War" *Time*, May 4, 2001.

Robert Kaylor, "At the Scene: How Guerrillas Pin Down a Soviet Ally," *U.S. News & World Report*, August 8, 1983.

Donald Kirk, "Vietnam Looks to the West," *New Leader*, July 25, 1988.

Colin Leinster, "Vietnam Revisited: Turn to the Right?" *Fortune*, August 1, 1988.

David Liebhold and Huw Watkin, "Cleaning Up the Beach," *Time International*, August 21, 2000.

Susanna McBee, "The Amerasians: Tragic Legacy of Our Far East Wars," *U.S. News & World Report*, May 7, 1984.

Terry McDermott, "Dollars, Memories Lure U.S. Businessmen to Vietnam," Knight-Ridder/Tribune News Service, February 14, 1994.

Stewart Powell, Robert S. Dudney, and Robert Kaylor, "Vietnam: The Lasting Impact," *U.S. News & World Report*, April 22, 1985.

Michael P. Smith and Bernadette Tarallo, "The Unsettling Resettlement of Vietnamese Boat People," *USA Today* magazine, March 1993.

Mike Tharp, "Divided Generations: Little Saigon Vietnamese-Americans Form Community in Westminster, California," *U.S. News & World Report*, July 17, 2000.

Time International, "The Kids Are All Right," August 21, 2000.

Peter Vilbig, "The New Rebels," *New York Times Upfront*, January 1, 2001.

Videos

Ian McLeod, producer, *Vietnam: The Ten Thousand Day War*. Toronto: Canadian Broadcasting Corporation, 1980. This highly informative twelve-episode series by Pulitzer Prize winner Peter Arnett was produced just a few years after the war ended and features comments from many of the chief participants spoken while the events were still quite fresh in their minds.

Sandy Northrop, producer, *Pete Peterson: Assignment Hanoi*. Boston: WGBH-TV, 1997. A look at the life of the first U.S. ambassador to Communist Vietnam, a former POW who spent several years in the infamous "Hanoi Hilton" prison camp.

Carole Peters, producer, *The Vietnam War: A Descent into Hell*. New York: Discovery Channel, 1999. A searing examination of the errors in judgment made by U.S. political leaders and military advisers, all of which culminated in U.S. troops landing in Da Nang in March 1965 to fight the Communists.

Judith Vecchione, producer, *Vietnam: A Television History*. Boston: WGBH-TV, 1983. No stone is left unturned in this important project, which runs some thirteen hours and adds valuable new insights into the Vietnam War.

Internet Sources

Avalon Project at Yale Law School, "Indochina—Vietnam, Cambodia, and Laos," 2002. www.yale.edu.

Agency France-Presse "Technology: Vietnam May Restrict Internet Access." The Nando Times, August 16, 2002. www.nandotimes.com.

Nick Farrell, "Vietnam Orders Internet Crackdown," Vnunet.com, August 20, 2002. www.vnunet.com.

The History Place, "United States in Vietnam 1945–1975," 1999. www.history place.com.

New York Times on the Web, "Vietnam Today: A Different War," 2000. www.nytimes.com.

U.S. State Department, "Foreign Relations Series Volumes Online," 2002. www.state.gov.

Mike Yamamoto, "Vietnam Issues Internet Restrictions," CNET News, June 4, 1996. www.cnetnews.com.

Index

Picture Credits

Cover Image: Associated Press, AP

© AFP/CORBIS, 99

Associated Press, AP, 45, 48, 52, 59, 70, 100

© Bettmann/CORBIS, 37, 67, 78, 81, 83, 85, 87

© Corel Corporation, 93, 105

© Dover Pictorial Archive, 28

© PAVLOVSKY JAQUES/CORBIS SYGMA, 64

© STONE LES/CORBIS SYGMA, 92, 107

© Library of Congress, 19, 21, 24, 26, 31, 34, 35, 40, 43, 50, 56, 74

© Wally McNamee/CORBIS, 89

© Francoise de Mulder/CORBIS, 61

© Tim Page/CORBIS, 73

© Reuters NewMedia Inc./CORBIS, 96

About the Author

Philip Gavin is a web publishing pioneer who founded The History Place (historyplace.com), one of the Internet's most beloved educational sites, visited by millions since 1996. Mr. Gavin has written extensively for the website on the rise of Adolf Hitler and the Holocaust, along with American history topics including the Vietnam War, and world history topics such as the Irish Potato Famine. In 2001, an article by Mr. Gavin on ethnic cleansing in Bosnia-Herzegovina was published in the book *Genocide*, an anthology from Greenhaven Press. Mr. Gavin also has a background in journalism and television. In 1994, he received an award for "Songs of the Season," a delightful children's holiday special. He lives in Quincy, Massachusetts.